D0854999

Pablo Ruiz Picasso, *The Young Painter*, 1972

Sheila Paine

Artists Emerging

Sustaining Expression
through Drawing

ASHGATE

Copyright © Ashgate, 2000
Text copyright © Sheila Paine, 2000
Illustrations copyright as per list of illustrations

The author has asserted her moral rights

All rights reserved. No part of this publication may be
reproduced, stored in a retrieval system, or transmitted
in any form or by any means electronic, mechanical,
photocopying, recording, or otherwise, without the prior
permission of the publisher

Published by
Ashgate Publishing Limited
Gower House
Croft Road
Aldershot
Hampshire GU11 3HR
England

Ashgate Publishing Company
131 Main Street
Burlington
VT 05401 – 5600
USA

British Library Cataloguing-in-Publication Data
Paine, Sheila
Artists emerging: sustaining expression through drawing
1. Child artists – Training of 2. Child artists – Psychology
3. Creation (Literary, artistic, etc) 4. Art – Study and
teaching – Philosophy 5. Artists – Training of – Philosophy
6. Creation (Literary, artistic, etc) – Psychological aspects
I. Title
704'.054

ISBN 0 7546 0200 1

Library of Congress Cataloging-in-Publication Data
Paine, Sheila.
    Artists emerging: sustaining expression through
    drawing/Sheila Paine.
      184 p. 24.6 cm
    Includes bibliographical references and index.
    ISBN 0–7546–0200–1 (HB)
      1. Child artists—Psychology. 2. Creative ability in
    children. 3. Drawing—Study and teaching. I. Title.
    N351.P24 2000
    704'.054–dc21   00–025721

Produced for the publisher by
John Taylor Book Ventures, Faringdon, Oxfordshire

Typeset in Palatino by
Tom Knott, Mears Ashby, Northampton

Illustrations scanned by
Welsh Offset Printers, Cwmbran

Printed in Belgium

Contents

N
351
·P24
2000

To my father, who first encouraged me to draw,
and to Toby, Charlotte, Elanwy, Victor, Ruby
and all other young people who draw so
splendidly, as well as those who encourage them

Illustrations

6 A savage and gentle passion

Except where otherwise stated, all drawings and paintings are on permanent loan to the Drumcroon Education Art Centre, Wigan, Lancashire; they are published here with the kind permission of the late artist.

7 The young humorist

All drawings and paintings © Annetta Hoffnung, published with her permission.

8 A professional journey

Except when stated otherwise, all drawings and paintings © Sarah Raphael, published with her permission and in the possession of the Raphael family.

9 Displacing the demon

All drawings © the Downes family, published with their permission.

Foreword
Tom Phillips RA

Every artist builds a myth of infancy to answer both for himself and others the insistent question 'How Did This Begin?' Picasso's claim that at the age of nine he could draw like Raphael is baseless rhetoric: of course he could not (and neither could Raphael). He was kick-started at a very early age into artistic ways of thinking and looking. Had he been orphaned and such goads and props removed, would he have become an artist just the same? Undoubtedly yes, for there is a level of gift that cannot be denied even if it is suffocated with advantages or stifled with deprivation. Somewhere always there is a child who hums a melody in a tune-less house or who draws angels on a wall on which no picture has ever hung.

I wrote out my own mythology (which hovers be-tween two extremes) in a picture-poem. Even to use those words gives a clue: what else was Rupert Bear, before I knew of Blake, but a picture-poem? Although it contains no lies, the art-historical Truth Police would soon penetrate my overselective story, and under in-terrogation I would have to ask for all sorts of early visual stimuli to be taken into account, the things that made my dark suburban home even in time of war a house of treasures. Although acknowledged or in-tended art was entirely absent, I would still have to admit to shards of beauty everywhere, from the linear tartan of a football pools coupon and the containers of household wares to things I actually collected for their graphic excitement, like matchbox labels and the packets which razor blades came in. Through these I could extrapolate the larger world of design.

If there is such an entity as the artistic spirit its first manifestation is as a search engine dedicated to truffling out relevant stuff from the most unpromising environment. Such an engine thus sent out to feed grows fit and is tirelessly at work while its possessor (unaware of the concept of art or the notion of an artist) still dreams of being a fireman or footballer. Once expression enters the equation another factor comes into play, the dissatisfaction machine, which shifts up a gear with every achievement. Teacher's praise or parent's pride (so satisfying to the normal child) cannot compete with the unsleeping critic in the tiny artist's head, which, as if Poe's raven had learnt Beckett's words, croaks, 'No matter. Try again, Fail again. Fail better.'

This book examines with finer analytic tools than I possess, the mysteries of artistic beginnings. But the parallels are always there and I encounter them in the initial chapters of any creative biography. The joy of learning is to find that one is not alone. I remember reading when I was about fifteen (and already con-demned or committed to the artistic life) in the note-books of Leonardo da Vinci his instruction to young painters to stare at stains on the wall and to find in them figures and fantastic landscapes. One thing a London house in wartime did not lack (for decoration was considered, if not merely wasteful, a challenge to fate) was blotchy wallpaper and plaster with spreading islands of damp. I unwittingly obeyed Leonardo by spending hour upon infant hour summoning up angels and demons amid tortuous clouds or craggy terrain, thinking somehow I was the only person peculiar enough to invent such worlds. Wonderful then to discover that this commonplace of fantasy was in fact an early professional engagement. Such thoughts of aloneness are part of the mythology, of course. We artists are a larger breed than is supposed and not all of us are practitioners. We invest in what we see and make it yield imaginative dividends for ourselves and, in the happy cases where the modes of expression meet the material of invention, for others.

Acknowledgements

More people have helped at different stages with the development of this book than I can list here; in naming a few I want to acknowledge them all. I am most grateful for the assistance of Joyce and Tony Curtis, Margaret Hine, Joan and Bert Isaac, Sylvia May, Mr and Mrs Edward Millais, Sir Ralph and Lady Babette Millais, William Newland, Cherry Rowlands, the Schroder family, Dr Lorna Selfe, Tony Stevens, Marjorie Vivian, Dr Malcolm Warner and Elizabeth Waters.

I am particularly grateful to Annetta Hoffnung for so much enthusiastic support and kindness over many years. I thank her, as well as Geoffroy Millais, others of the Millais family, Madame du Vignaud de Villefort, members of the Tapié de Céleyran family, Sam Rothenstein, Frederic and Sylvia Raphael and Diana and Dave Downes for allowing me access to their collections.

Part of the research was funded through the award of a Fellowship by the Leverhulme Trust and two other phases of it by the Guild of St George.

It was also supported over several years by the London University Institute of Education, through the presentation in its Bedford Way Gallery in 1981 of the exhibition *Six Children Draw*, which I arranged (a book of the same name was published by the indulgent Roger Farrand, then of Academic Press) and through my always-stimulating contacts with its students and my staff colleagues. I owe a particular debt to my erstwhile Head of Department, Stanislav Frenkiel, whose rigorous and scholarly supervision of the doctoral work from which this book grew taught me many things I ought to have known about art and the use of language. More recently, with Pamela Edwardes of Scolar Press, I have enjoyed productive discussion on the content and final form of the book. Betty Blandino gave of her time to cast a critical but empathetic eye over the text.

I wish that John Everett Millais, Henri de Toulouse-Lautrec, Pablo Picasso and Gerard Hoffnung were here to thank for the rich delights of their early drawings; those have at least made me feel that they still are around. I hope that I sufficiently conveyed my gratitude to Michael Rothenstein while that most generous and perceptive of artists was alive. And I am able to express my warmest gratitude directly to Sarah Raphael and David Downes for their great assistance, interest and friendship.

Help has also been gratefully received from the Musée de Toulouse-Lautrec, Albi; the Picasso Museums in Barcelona and Paris; and the Royal Academy and Tate Gallery libraries in London.

Introduction

The happy few possess what Baudelaire calls 'impeccable naivete', the ability to see the world always afresh, either in its tragedy or in its hope. For the happy few, art and life are indistinguishable.

Anita Brookner, 'Jacques-Louis David: A Personal Interpretation' (1974)

Fifty years ago the English art educator and poet Herbert Read advocated that education should create artists in the sense of 'people efficient in the various modes of expression'. In the ensuing half-century his Platonic vision of a fundamentally aesthetic education, harmonising individuality within social unity, has flared like a beacon to many educators. It still reads as a powerful polemic, casting its light uncomfortably into the more regressive areas of current educational practice.[1] Central to this book is an investigation, in the specific context of visual art, of a way of fulfilling this important aim: through increasing our understanding of the circumstances and strategies that contribute to the earliest artistic development of those who become professional artists.

The greatest marvel of the world is human individuality, and perhaps its most puzzling aspect is that certain individuals accomplish remarkable things of which others appear incapable. This puzzle is most deeply evident in the context of the arts, whose images affect and even dominate our daily existence: how and why artists present their particular kinds of images to us is a matter of much speculation and confusion.

Yet the creation of art is a deep influence on our cultures and artists are the heroic instigators of that influence. We idolize some of them, though not necessarily during their lifetimes, and enthusiastically revile others. They constantly claim our attention, whether openly through exhibitions and critical acclaim or covertly by their subtle influences on the world we inhabit.

There is a daunting mythology about artistic skill and its value, especially concerning the ways in which it is acquired and developed, a mythology which determines our cultural relationship to the arts and the access that is provided to its pleasures and practice. Why some individuals become artists is a mystery not only of art but of history, psychology and mythology. Family background and educational opportunity seem to offer insufficient explanations for the remarkable and often rapid development of strong artistic fluency. We prefer to romanticize on the idea of the eminent artist as the recipient of a 'gift' from God or the gods, someone whose inherited eccentric personality explains the otherwise unexplainable. Creatively imagined in fiction (like 'Gulley Jimson' in Joyce Cary's *The Horse's Mouth* (1944)) or in reality in accounts of Bruckner, Byron or Braque, the artist seems an increasingly different kind of being.

Many individuals who show exceptional skill in artistic creation do seem to have been empowered from the beginning, as though (and according to the most enduringly popular notion) they have been specially selected and equipped prior to birth. Such a view assumes some kind of a break in the continuum of human facility; there would have to be these special people and then all the others.

The performance of those highest achievers to whom we apply the term 'genius' ('special inborn faculty', 'consummate intellectual, creative or other power, more exalted than talent', according to the Chambers *Twentieth Century Dictionary*) is astonishing and apparently inexplicable. Like the 'Midwich Cuckoos' of John Wyndham's fiction, they turn up in their earthly 'nests' without warning. Sometimes lacking any obvious hereditary explanation and frequently even without encouragement, they astound by their obsession and developing ability, launching into a relentless, thrusting career independent of an employer and continuing until death, ignoring all impediments.

Some, like fiery comets, burn out at an early stage from the sheer debilitation which their obsession induces. Others by skill or fortune sustain intermittent peaks of high achievement over a long creative life.

Is the artist-genius some kind of divine or genetic variation of the human system, extraordinary to the point of abnormality, or rather an example of highly accentuated development of an individual's capacities in a particular area of human achievement? The answer to this question is important because it places the genius and the work either outside or within the framework of normal human development and determines an isolation from or a relationship to other less spectacular practitioners and learners. 'Great' art could consequently appear inherently detached from ordinary life, as indeed some would argue it is – an inaccessible mystery, befitting the mystery surrounding its makers. While the development of great artistic ability seems unstoppable for the 'gifted' few, most people will thereby be considered divinely or genetically excluded from the attainment of such excellence or from its effects.

If such separate genius exists, how do we account for the diverse levels of excellence represented by individuals in our society? It is not just that there are these apparently very special people. It is also that some of *them* seem more accomplished than others, with the lesser practitioners bearing some relation in what they do to others not apparently 'endowed', who have nevertheless been able to develop high degrees of skill over a period of time, through study and practice. The spectrum of achievement from the strongest to the weakest seems to be continuous.

If the distinctive condition of genius is a fallacy, does no one in fact begin life especially endowed? Could *anyone* in theory attain any level of achievement through sufficient endeavour and the quick grasping of skills, even if these are mediated by the effects of family background, social contacts, education and access to the culture of the time? The sheer spectral range of artistic achievement makes this view hard to accept. But it is possible to imagine that the potential for degrees of higher achievement exists in everyone, even if it remains unobserved and little developed in most. This is an exciting view if we think of what the effects of unlocking such potential (the educator's great dream) could be, or a frustrating one if we consider that to be impossible.

It is not an unreasonable theory. Since Freud posited the existence of an ever-active unconscious area of cerebral activity in all of us and Jung emphasized its creative nature, it has been possible to envisage conscious thinking as the smaller and perhaps the least complex part of thinking in general. Why would it be so strange if abilities common to all were internalized in the unconscious, as part of an innate legacy of the totality of human experience, and if it were developed or not in each individual life according to circumstances? Such a theory does, however, raise all sorts of questions about the psychological and environmental forces which might, in combination, be determining the range of individual performance.

The weakness in this second view of exceptional performance is that there seems no reason to suppose that anything inherited is equally strongly inherited, any more than that physical attributes are equal in the newborn. A more plausible proposition, to which this investigation adheres, is that there are different levels or patterns of inherited disposition, still exceeding what most of us will probably utilize, which interact with the different forms of experience an individual encounters. That would explain the infinite diversity between individuals as well as the high achievements of some of them: so much difference in performance and in achievement may well derive from the tension generated between inner strengths and outer encounters. Individuals who are remarkable from the outset, others succeeding from a lowly start, those who strive or do not and those who succeed or do not may all be accommodated within such a proposition.

By definition this view brings the achievements of 'great' artists into the realm of everyone, by arguing, not that such achievement is likely for all, but that all manifestations of it are related. That relationship is sometimes less than clear, even as between mature individuals, and it is particularly unclear in the case of the work of younger as compared with older individuals. Yet artistic development is from the beginning a continuous process, within which ideas grow, skills develop and personal visions are formed. It is therefore fascinating to enquire how the development of high achievers compares from the earliest stages with that of others and what, if any, predictions can reasonably be made.

If high-achieving professionals have reached that position through their earlier intuitive development of effective strategies for progress, could their examples, together with those of others less spectacular, provide guidance to opening up the facility for many more people? The remoteness of many individuals from the arts suppresses a major avenue for expression and judgement affecting their quality of life. Individuals and societies would benefit if more people could describe their feelings and meanings through art, and could also understand the expressive forms of others. Strengths in artistic expression are as essential to personal fulfilment as the capability for expression through speech. Such abilities do not make for perfect beings, but they unlock capabilities of response that are denied to many.

To avoid any religious and symbolic as well as divisive connotations of the term 'genius', and to emphasize the continuing-spectrum model of artistic development and achievement I am embracing here, higher achievers in the arts at any level will normally be described in what follows as 'exceptional' (in the sense of 'unusual'). The image of the artist I employ here is a contemporary one (although it seems to me it has always been relevant): as S. Moholy-Nagy (expressing the view of Paul Klee) put it, as 'more than a refined camera … a child of this earth; yet also child of the Universe'.[2]

I have so far spoken mainly of the arts in general and shall continue to do so when appropriate; sometimes the term 'artist' is used to mean poet, writer, actor or composer as well as painter, sculptor or printmaker. But my focus is on visual art, primarily two-dimensional, and it is inclined towards drawing as constant and central to art. Many lively and seductive images lie at the heart of this investigation; as many as possible, constituting only a few from the many available, have been included.

The investigation is soft-focused. Eschewing any scientific method and accepting the mystery which is art, it seeks to illuminate (rather than to prove) the potential relevance to everyone of fluency in expressive drawing and therefore of the successful strategies of the developing artist. While, for reasons of clarity, the term 'artist' is normally used to refer to those for whom art was or becomes a career, Read's wider application of it to all who work expressively at any age is tacitly recognized throughout. The need of the prodigious for strong, positive, timely and effective support is argued also to be the need of *any* individual. However, the educational model I have favoured here, though valuing the practice of art, is one which acts through the expressive imagination rather than centring on systems and techniques.

Using examples of specific children and artists, in Chapter 1 I examine the image of the child in history, for its bearing upon attitudes to children's drawing, as activity, skill, expression and art, and review some consequences of different perceptions of the relevance of artistic skill to the young learner. Beliefs about tutoring and curricula priorities, the degree of access to study, sources of funding and the value attributed to art itself, are all seen as reflected in the differing forms of past or existing systems of art training.

Chapter 2 examines artistic and biographical causes for the success of that small minority of individuals who develop the strongest fluency in drawing, art and expression. Traditional interpretations of success, strength and progression are challenged. Examples from the experience of artists (of all kinds) help to reveal some of the circumstances and also the nature of the condition of being or becoming an artist, as do some examples of failure to fulfil earlier promise and, conversely, the late development of artistic skill. Cases of fluent drawing among the young mentally impaired call into question our attitudes to early fluency in art and to the way in which we think we can generate quicker assimilation of artistic skills. They also challenge assumptions about links between 'autist' (my own term) and artist which will be revisited in two of the case-studies below.

Subsequent chapters contrast the early drawings and the lives of seven individuals who have matured as artists. Selected from a limited number of cases I have identified and researched, they present important contrasts of situation, support, personality, development and achievement. Three of those selected were born in the nineteenth century, and the others in the twentieth; their countries of origin include France, Spain, Germany and the United Kingdom; their family backgrounds range from the wealthy to the modest. Seen in the context of a wider eclectic view of development in the arts, they explore a range of phenomena – personal, environmental and educational – which impinge upon it.

The most eminent artist discussed here, Picasso, is included because of his unique awareness of the art of the child and his own desire to recapture its essence, significantly embodying that desire in *The Young Painter* (1972; see frontispiece), shortly before he died. Millais and Toulouse-Lautrec share with him the similar experience of a rigorous nineteenth-century academic training, managing to sustain their own style, interests and vision alongside it. Michael Rothenstein and Sarah Raphael are artists of the twentieth century, both brought up in art-conscious households, encouraged but not dominated by support and teaching. The work of Gerard Hoffnung, a master of caricature, shows just how soon particular interests can develop and culture be influential, while the drawings of the initially impaired David Downes continue to be instruments for the diffusion of fears and the protection of emotion.

The final chapter surveys the implications of these studies together with the examples raised in Chapter 2, extending our picture of the evolving artist and helping to reveal some of the strategies adopted (knowingly or intuitively) to further development. No single pattern emerges but there are correspondences, notably concerning the adoption of successive styles, the emergence of persistent themes, the awareness of artistic traditions, as well as the intellectual or therapeutic relevance of the works to their makers, and the disposition to become 'artistic' as well as the tensions between convention and individuality which fuel this obsession.

The emergent phenomenon I describe is early obsessive drawing, which is naturally more concerned with experiment than with representation and the most important part of which is spontaneous, eclectic and constantly re-inventive. By its very flexibility and diversity it seems to be an intuitive preparation for fending off subsequent discouraging pressures as well as an investment towards future achievement. But the whole process of artistic development appears to be vulnerable, even in the initially able and particularly in the less resilient. Self-image and individuality can be sacrificed or wasted at any stage, through inflexible, inappropriate, untimely or inadequate support.

I conclude by offering some proposals for the guidance of those who assist enthusiastic and highly motivated young people. I argue that the difficulties which others with less initial facility encounter are amenable to fundamentally similar strategies and that their right to such opportunity is as strong. While successful artists are not perfect beings, they have acquired a powerful attribute: an expressive fluency which can make their relationship to the culture around them deeper and more autonomous, a condition with obvious value, not just for aspiring professionals (Brookner's 'happy few') but for everyone.

In some still inaccessible but interactive fusion of nature and nurture lies an ultimate explanation for artistic development. For that inaccessibility we should be grateful: mysteries are wonderful things and they evade the potential banality of clear descriptions.

Historical attitudes to the young as artists

We are travelling away all the time from childhood and from our own past and there is something deeply reassuring about the discovery of roots to show how it all began ... it's all to do with energy and tracing the source of that energy.

Michael Rothenstein, in a catalogue preface (1989)

The seriousness of children's art

The twentieth century has often been described as the century of the child, at least for the affluent and educated areas of the world. The majority of children in those areas consequently received care and attention. The state took an active interest in their physical development and in the prevention of childhood diseases. Children were protected from exploitation by laws which regulated their employment and in ways which would have been inexplicable to societies in preceding centuries. They were the subject of considerable and expensive educational provision, whatever may be thought of its nature and quality. Special clothes were designed and made for their use, intricate and often costly toys were available for them and hours of entertaining film and video productions catered for their interests. Play activities were seen as natural and sometimes as educative.

Juvenile art in the century just ended suffered from its image as play. Few adults think that a child might work hard to create a drawing. Such an activity, however much developed, is rarely credible even as a preparation for an artistic career, let alone as intrinsically valuable. Because the images drawn by children are different from those of adults, they may be judged inept and without real value now or in the future, even when they are presented in prestigious ways in the very few museums devoted to the work of children. And even though some psychologists and pedagogues have written quite extensively about 'child art', it has mainly been artists themselves who have been concerned with the child's 'aesthetic inventiveness'.[1]

In European societies, attitudes are beginning to change and the example of the life and work of the twentieth century's greatest artist, Picasso, is proving instrumental in that. Probably no other artist in history has had so much written about him by so many authors and so rapidly, both during and after his life. This astonishing coverage also includes analysis of the formative role of his earliest work in childhood and adolescence.

As the most prominent twentieth-century artist, Picasso is a phenomenon of a time when being a child had greater social and cultural significance than in previous centuries. Repression of the young had given way to indulgence, discipline to permission, with the earlier limitations of school-based learning opened up by new technology.

So far these changes have had slight effect upon prevailing opinions of children's art, even though art has a curriculum place in the schools of many nations. Nor have changed attitudes yet generated much new interest in the early works of most contemporary artists. There are certainly a few collections of artistic juvenilia in museums and a few which are from individual artists, but these usually have a low profile. A museum in Herefordshire stores the drawings of Brian Hatton (1887–1916) by subject-matter rather than chronologically; age and stage are considered unimportant. The juvenilia of Picasso form the big exception. While smaller amounts are stored in Paris, mainly in archives rather than on show, the bulk of his earliest production forms a massive and superbly documented chronological display in the Barcelona Picasso Museum. Picasso was the main instigator of this situation.

It is not just the existence of this collection which may be changing opinion. A second factor is the knowledge of Picasso's attitudes to his own childhood work in particular and to children's art in general. This is more widely discussed in a later part of this book, but it matters here to note the prominence that has been given to his comments in these respects, to what is widely known of the influence upon him of the various exhibitions of child art held in London and in Paris in the 1920s and to the clear evidence from his own mature work and development in support of the attitudes he expressed.

A few other artists have now responded to his lead. In preparing in 1989 for a retrospective exhibition of his own life's work as painter and printmaker, the artist Michael Rothenstein found it appropriate to reflect on the kind of journey on which artists embark. Recent interest shown in the extensive records of his own early work made him more aware than before of its relevance to his later work and even affected the nature of it.

For writers on art, the phrase 'the formative years' usually still means the years post-adolescence, but the words and work of Picasso are instigating a new perception of the significance of that phrase for earlier art activity.

Between art and the work of children

That this new dawning has not spread outwards to encourage the valuing of early work from many more historical and contemporary artists may be due paradoxically to some inhibiting factors in otherwise potentially encouraging developments of the last century. The very explosion of interest in the art of ordinary children which generated the exhibitions (in Britain, France, Austria and America between 1908 and 1938) that were so influential upon Picasso and his contemporaries gave form to the notion that 'child art' was actually a special kind of art with its own characteristics and qualities, not readily to be evaluated in relation to art in general. While child art, by being so defined in the twentieth century, achieved a separate status for itself and for its promotion as a worthwhile activity for children and in schools, the art of children lost much of the value it might have had in the context of art in general.[2]

The separation from art implicit in the term 'child art', and the hint of inferiority which it conveys, has clearly been a welcome notion for some, for whom a closer connection is perceived as potentially threatening to art itself. Edward Robinson, in a letter to *Modern Painters* (Winter 1992), wrote that:

no doubt links can sometimes be traced between great art and the play of infancy. But if one believes … that human beings can be distinguished from all other species by their capacity for a spiritual vision that can change the world (otherwise why should the arts be felt to be such a threat to the established order?), this identification of art with its origins in

childhood can only trivialise its nature and undermine its authority, and will ultimately play into the hands of those reactionaries who want to see the arts kept in their place.[3]

A second and inherently damaging development was the plethora of initiatives to evaluate art as opposed to valuing it. For the last 90 years and more, the art of children has become a victim of the scrutinizing sciences; children's imagery has been intellectually dismembered, with their drawings analysed fragmentally rather than for their whole natures and meanings. In some research, forms and marks have been interpreted as number-equivalents in the hope of arriving at meaningful descriptions of the learning development of their makers. The expression of children's ideas as illustration or symbolism has been taken as evidence of their personalities or their psychological problems. This has contrived to distort the general view of children's art and achievement. And it certainly has not helped in the appraisal of the emerging talent of the young artist-to-be, whose dynamic and often unusual surges of progression seem to contradict the concepts of rigid and inflexible sequences which have been the theoretical outcome of many of the formal investigations.

Anthropology and psychology have emerged only within the last century and a half to reappraise our understanding of human nature and behaviour and to create new vantage points for the examination of human experience and achievement.[4] Charles Darwin's 1877 study of the development of his own child must be regarded as a remarkable precursor of these disciplines.[5] Luquet's study of his daughter's drawing, however, seems almost to victimize her rather than to celebrate her mind.[6] Being both controversial and imperfectly understood in many sectors of contemporary society, the consequences of the new sciences have been reactive as well as initiating, reinforcing some of the oldest attitudes towards the social perception of art and children. Philosophy, on the other hand, has drawn new attention to the processes of intuition which affect much of our understanding of the visual and the aesthetic.[7]

In particular, the twentieth century, like no other, has seen art as the focus of a pitched and unresolved battle between the proponents of a new ideology for the arts and the resolute supporters of tradition, or at any rate of the perceived tradition. Hilton Kramer described the twentieth-century development in art by which the medium became a major factor in the nature of the art image:

no longer did the subject enjoy an unchallenged authority in determining either the aesthetic character of a painting … the subject … was no longer the centre of emotional gravity which had shifted to the properties of the medium that had never before been so intensely and unremittingly scrutinised for their inherent expressive powers or given such priority in painting.[8]

Nowhere is the battle more fierce than in the issue of the apparent presence or absence in an artist's work of those formal skills, largely representational, which were once the prime mark of artistic excellence. Being concerned to effect a different kind of expression, the Modernist (quite reasonably) sees no need to demonstrate them in any structured or visually explicit way, though some critics may feel that he should.

This controversy extends into the arena of children's education, where a child's most natural expressive manner, derived from a combination of direct sensation and as yet unsullied vision, is so frequently seen as evidence of temporary incompetence rather than of different perceptions, methods and objectives that are appropriate to a child. To succeed in art, it is assumed that one must pass through a long process of formal learning of accredited skills. From that point of view the art of children cannot be considered seriously, given that it emerges from such comparatively short periods of often untutored experience. In a reported occurrence in England in 1992, a four-year-old child's painting was accepted for an exhibition as being the work of an adult; the important issue was taken by many to be about whether the selectors had been duped, rather than about the degree of artistic achievement represented by the child's work.

There is little question that professional training, through apprenticeship (like that of the medieval artist) or schooling, is customarily valuable to becoming an artist, even though it guarantees nothing about quality and even though many students of art have become artists by reacting against much of the teaching they received (many teachers would agree that good teaching is provocative rather than dominant). But the history of art is full of examples of artists accepted as such who are known to be self-taught, of late-developing untrained artists and even of children displaying advanced drawing skills normally associated with tuition. The French Post-Impressionist Paul Gauguin had no formal artistic training, and little is on record of his earliest art activity until he is identified as 'a Sunday painter' at the age of 23 and being informally tutored by his guardian's daughter. He appears to have avoided tuition by attending life-drawing classes at a small atelier rather than at the Ecole des Beaux-Arts.[9] Nothing is known of drawings he might have done as a younger person, nor of the earlier drawing activity, if any there was, of the 'primitive' late-comer to art Alfred Wallis (1855–1942). Tuition is not necessarily an experience by which one

defines the artist. Nor it seems is age; if the art of the untaught may sometimes be art, then so also may be the work of children, even though they are acting, as most do, at different conceptual and practical levels.

Such conclusions would not have been acceptable while the state of childhood was undervalued. But if the evidence from art itself is valid, the change in attitudes to childhood has not been one of simple transition from ignorance to awareness or from low to high status, nor has the change in the treatment of children been a simple passage from neglect to care or from control to freedom; the patterns are more in the nature of fluctuation than of linear progression.

The ways in which children have been portrayed in art can suggest contemporary social attitudes towards them. Velázquez's portraits of infant princesses of the Spanish royal family make them look as though childhood was something they were never permitted to experience; Picasso's *Boy with a Dove* appears unlikely to grow up or perhaps (already possessing a child's clear view of the world) to need to grow up. It is intriguing to note that Giotto, in the early fourteenth century, portrayed children as having bodies of near-adult proportions, denying their childish state, while Pompeian murals of some fifteen centuries earlier show (winged) children drawn with realistic body proportions as though being a child was well understood.

Early training in art

While there could be many reasons for the differences in the ways artists have portrayed children, and by inference childhood, such changes may have oscillated because of the roles which some children could usefully play in their society. An account of one of the earliest examples of the provision of art education for children refers to an unspecified period of ancient Egyptian history:

How great was the care and pedagogical skill the Egyptians expended on young artists is shown by the teaching materials which have been preserved, the plaster casts from nature, the anatomical representations of individual parts of the body intended for instructional purposes and above all, those specimen showpieces, which demonstrated to the pupils the development of the work of art in all the phases of its production.[10]

There is certainly some evidence for this assertion. It has been reasonably established that young children in the village of Dahr el Medina, which existed in the Valley of the Kings near Luxor at the time of some of the greatest tomb decoration, were trained as artists;[11] their literary learning was also regarded as important and is said to be very obvious from the nature of their later imagery. Colour palettes have been found, with too many colours present to make them relevant only to writing activities, in the tombs of those who died quite young. But ages are not given and teaching methods are not known; the artefacts that Hauser describes do exist but have no necessary connection with very young artists.

The evidence is enough, however, to provide a picture of a society that valued a few of its children for their potential and invested time in training them. This general picture recurs in the history of childhood, particularly in connection with the arts. Hauser also describes how young artists were trained in the monastic workshops of early medieval Europe: 'In many monasteries ... handicraft workshops were set up which served primarily educational purposes and guaranteed ... a constant supply of young artists.'[12] Again, it is not quite clear just how young such students were, although they do seem to have been educated as much for their value as individuals as for their working potential, an attitude that is historically unusual. Another account, of the teaching in the workshops of Italian artists of the fourteenth century, states that 'they were apprenticed to a master while still children and spent many years with him'. Hauser argues that these children were seen as useful for their skill more than they were valued as individuals, even though teaching methods were more individual: 'for these boys are if not the best, at least the cheapest source of labour; and that is probably the main reason for the more intensive art education which is to be observed from now on'.[13]

Hauser does not comment on the general absence of children as subjects for artists rather than merely as apprentices to art. While the subject-matter of Egyptian art was heavily determined by the status of mature individuals and provision for their after-lives, one can read no significance into the general lack of children as such in their art. But in medieval art, the secondary presence given to children as minor deities, heirs or attendants does seem to endorse Hauser's belief in the unimportance of children generally, as does the manner of drawing children, with adult-proportioned bodies, which seems to reflect a failure to accept or a wish to ignore childhood. And on the use of children in the making of art, it seems clear that they were, to the Egyptians and later, essentially partially skilled labourers whose own approaches to drawing and to expression were quite irrelevant. Only in the monasteries of Europe did the founding of schools and orphanages demonstrate an unusual concern for the interests of children well beyond their possible future value as priests.

By the late sixteenth century the training of children in the workshops of artists appears to have become conventional practice in some European countries, although there are possible instances much earlier than that; both Leonardo and Michelangelo are known to have trained young men in painting and sculpture in their studios, though the age of these trainees at the start of their training is uncertain. But in Italy, for example, the artist Ludovico Carracci (1555–1619) founded a teaching academy in Bologna 'which became the most celebrated of its kind and was responsible for the training of most major Bolognese painters of the next generation';[14] a contemporary engraving shows that some of the pupils at work in the academy's studios may have been only five or six years of age (fig.1.1).

Clearly, among some artists at least, there was a belief that an early training was important and that it could not begin too soon (although apprenticeships in craftsmen's guilds generally had tended to begin later, at around fifteen years). It was not a belief likely to be shared by those who at that time saw childhood as a brief period of indulged infantile behaviour from which, at around seven years, an individual was expected to step straight into adulthood.[15] In this 'coddling' concept of childhood (the term means 'to pamper' or 'to warm an egg slowly'), children were free to behave as they wished without control. Childhood activity and the tasks of adult life had no positive connection; to train a child in adult skills of any kind would have been deemed unrealistic. Brueghel's sixteenth-century portrayal of a Flemish *Wedding Feast* clearly expresses this view: the children present at the feast are onlookers, eating and playing separately; they do not sit at table and take no part in the preparations or the serving. Perhaps this was not the whole picture of childhood. In Tudor England, for example, there is some evidence that, where it was expedient, small children were trained in handicrafts to put their time to profitable use, but with no intention to prepare them for any later adult livelihood.

The early training in Carracci's academy predated the emergence of a second concept of childhood which seems to have arisen in Europe in the seventeenth century as an exasperated reaction to the behaviour generated and permitted by the first. Children were thought to be 'unready' for life rather than just waiting to become old enough to participate fully in it. They needed a form of training which would induct them into that part of knowledge which carried cultural approval. Whether that need was fulfilled or even recognized in individual cases was largely a matter of social status.

Society benefited from the practical outcomes of

1.1 Odoardo Fialetti, *The Academy of Design at Carracci's Academy in Bologna*, an illustration in *Gli esordi dei Carracci e gli affreschi di Palazzo Fava* (Bologna: Nuovo Alfa Editoriale, n.d.)

this second perception of childhood in so far as those deemed to be children (male children, at least, and a chronologically extended group) were kept away from adult society and sent to school, or tutored, for longer periods of time instead of being indulged. Concerning the study and practice of art, it became acceptable to envisage such training as valuable beyond the training of future artists, as part of a general education. Though based on theory rather than experience, Rousseau's description of the role of drawing in the education of his imaginary eighteenth-century pupils is a natural development of this view. 'Emile' would not have been pressed to learn to read before the age of twelve (assuming he would then teach himself) but would have been encouraged to draw well before that age, as a means to the training of his perceptions,[16] an echo of

a view of the arts first proposed by Aristotle, who saw them as powerful influences in the building of character. Emile's female counterpart 'Sophie' would also draw, but in her case because drawing is 'closely connected with taste in dress'.[17]

One might assume that any extension of the availability of training in drawing and art would be likely to benefit the cause of the early training of artists generally; the more these studies featured in the curriculum, the more children of high potential ought to have encountered them. The reality, of course, was that wealthy families had access to good schooling or good tutoring and a liberal education which emphasized cultural induction, cultural values and the arts; for other children, where they were fortunate enough to encounter continuous education at all, art played little part and drawing was taught as a manipulative and disciplinary skill. Crafts were taught to quite small children in eighteenth-century Britain, but only so that they could work at repetitive tasks in small cottage industries.

A century later, when the working-class child was extracted from a factory or labouring role to be educated, this was in order to receive a range of vocationally oriented skills which involved copying exercises and discouraged imaginative response. Thus in Britain, as in many other European countries, the chance to become an artist by early training was biased towards children from wealthier families, possibly more than in the days when fortunate exceptional children such as Giotto could be extracted from a lowly existence and apprenticed in a workshop or studio.

Tutoring at home

As the concept of the child had gradually changed, so, by the time of the Renaissance, had the social idea of the artist. Unlikely to be of poor background, no longer an artisan who served an apprenticeship, the artist became a person, usually male, whose family could afford to be financially supportive and to provide such training as seemed necessary to achieve professional standards. Since being artistic had become culturally correct as one of the ways to demonstrate social superiority, the skills of the artist were generally practised in such families as amateur accomplishments (even by women) and art tutors might be employed even when a career as an artist was not intended. Many future artists of the eighteenth and nineteenth centuries began to draw and paint, apparently, because it was a family custom and a social attribute. Parents, even if they were not artists themselves, would revere the display of fluent visual expression and encourage it, just as soon as it sufficiently emulated adult performance.

The issue of emulation is important on at least two counts. First, prior to the twentieth century (and to an extent within it too), there was rarely interest in a child's drawing activity until it appeared to imitate traditionally accepted methods, styles and subject-matter. This is borne out by many of the available collections of individual drawing development, which usually begin at around six or seven years when the child's imagery was in adult terms well formed; the earlier, 'lesser' drawings which were no doubt made were rarely saved. Secondly, in the case of girls, as Germaine Greer notes, direct imitation of parents' own work was usually the only way for female children to sustain encouragement, given that such children were

unwelcome as independent artists, however talented they seemed.[18] Greer does not say so, but the situation seems to have been similar for many boys, who had also initially to imitate – and in their case eventually to evade – a parent's artistic style.

A family taking early ability seriously might provide an art tutor, with tuition more likely to have been directed at dilettante accomplishment than at making a living as an artist. But if a major artistic fluency was particularly valued, it was seen to be never too soon to provide tutoring in order to accelerate development; the ability was deemed to need early structuring. Rarely were hired art tutors very eminent as artists in their own right, although they may have been good teachers of the principles and favoured practices of drawing of their time. It is arguable in individual cases whether their tuition was beneficial or detrimental; the strongest pupils probably adopted and rejected advice according to their own clear sense of purpose and direction. The role of the tutor was often to make the pupil capable of jumping the admission hurdles put up by training institutions, whose arbitrary requirements were well known. The entry requirements were less likely to identify individuality than to pick out those who had been conventionally disciplined.

European academies of art

Before the nineteenth century, the most promising young students of art in western Europe would have been likely to present themselves for admission to one of the major art academies, initially Italian ones in Florence, Perugia and Rome. In the seventeenth century, the Académie Française (eventually known as the Académie des Beaux-Arts) in Paris was formed in imitation of the Roman Accademia di San Luca and was adjudged by many to be the most prestigious of them all because of the direction and rigour of its teaching. After the abandonment in the nineteenth century of some of the Classical tradition and its replacement with all the tumultuous activity of the Romantic movement, what remained of that tradition was an extremely high standard in the teaching of drawing, covering the study of anatomy, perspective, design and life drawing. Later new European academies adopted similar teaching styles and tried to emulate its standards.

The privately sponsored British Royal Academy, formed in the mid-eighteenth century and a major centre for training artists, is of particular interest in the context of early teaching for young artists, as it chose to admit some extremely young students and to teach them alongside some fairly mature ones. The idea of a right age of 'readiness' to study anything and a rigid age-hierarchy applied to school systems is of largely European origin; Asian educational systems, for example, have traditionally formed teaching groups on the basis of need or stage of development rather than of age, with broad representation of ages in any group. It is no accident that, in the English educational system, it was art training which first challenged age-based teaching structures, for it is in the study of art that most difficulties are encountered in finding a logical sequence for what may be taught.

The Royal Academy did have a rigid teaching sequence but that had little to do with any notion of how learning develops. It was an arbitrary and pro-fessionally reinforced sequence of admissions to the drawing of different subjects, with drawing from the Antique at its base and life drawing at its pinnacle. To gain admission to its Schools, everyone took the same examination. The very young usually needed to attend an art 'crammer' preparatory school, the curriculum of which was tightly directed towards performance in the specified examination tasks and primarily concerned with drawing from parts of Antique figures: a foot, an arm, a head or a decorative architectural border. The Royal Academy was happy to consider entrants of ten or eleven years, such as the young Millais (see Chapter 3), as well as those in their forties.

The pattern in France and Spain in the nineteenth century seems to have been similar, if the sequence was differently timed. Paris had a number of smaller schools where youngsters such as the young Toulouse-Lautrec could attend to work in the life studio or from the Antique; he was twelve when he enrolled there. Picasso studied nepotistically in his father's art school until, at the age of fourteen, he was accepted for the Llotja School of Fine Arts in Barcelona; his father may have delayed entering him there because of his desire to maintain control over him.

The young of wealthy or influential families were usually the beneficiaries of these systems (particularly in Britain), which for a long time remained flexible enough to permit the tuition of some students who were no more than children. The desirability of such early acceleration of training, in terms of the well-being of the individual as well as of ultimate achievement, was unquestioned. The worth of the actual courses for any student was only occasionally criticized. The English nineteenth-century painter Frith noted in his autobiography of 1887 that many who won the Academy's medals for good achievement disappeared from view as artists when they left the Schools, while others who had been more independent there achieved later eminence;[19] these comments applied as much to older admissions as to some who started very young.

It is worth noting that the increasing number of public art schools set up in Britain in the nineteenth century at last created opportunities for women to study art. At the peak of this development, the Glasgow School of Art actually had several women on its staff by the end of the century, though there was little opportunity for young girls to study art. Professional opportunities for women generally remained few; a career decorating ceramics in the Doulton workshops, such as that adopted by the painter Kate Rogers (1861–1942), was only just re-spectable and, as in her case, marriage (for her in 1895) often caused the cessation of working as an artist.

Art and specialism in contemporary education

In the twentieth century, developments in art and in education have reflected changes in what is thought desirable as art training for exceptionally able children, and indeed for children in general. The major Euro-pean academies continue to provide for the more advantaged students but, because of changes in the nature of general schooling, those under eighteen years of age are rarely eligible for admission. Home tutoring has become rare; a few parents pay for private instruc-tion when school provision seems inadequate. And off the back of some until recently popular educational theories, quite a strong if minor consensus view has developed that even the highly able are better off without formal art teaching.

Increases in state school provision broadened curricula there and initially rendered the study of art less vocational and more open to cultural influences than it had been before. Children were given oppor-tunities for visual expression as well as observation, for imaginative experiment as well as disciplined rehearsal of skills. The proportion of the former to the latter is questionable and has been dependent upon individual schools and teachers, but it has meant that the art skills taught in schools had less to do with discipline and more to do with art as creative and imaginative, as well as having at least some tenuous relationship with contemporary artistic developments.

Expanded state school systems in most Western countries had no positive policy for the nurturing of exceptional art skills; for a long time that was left to chance, on the assumption that transfer to an art school was early enough at the age of sixteen or later. This meant that for young students with exceptional artistic fluency, the time spent on art studies was insufficient to nourish their skills. In some schools, too, eventual transfer from school to art school had an inferior status to transferring to university, reflecting a general judge-ment of art as a less prestigious field of study.

Recent early training initiatives

In spite of the general move in Western education towards a long-overdue leavening of opportunity for all children, the idea of a need for accelerated and dedicated study for some individuals remained alive. The provision for the very young pioneered by the more élitist and sometimes privately funded academies was replicated in new forms in several countries, even where a growing socialist philosophy and power might have determined otherwise. Nowhere is this development more surprising than under the now-extinct Soviet-Communist regime. In Moscow and Leningrad (now St Petersburg) schools focusing on a variety of subject specialisms were set up for the education of highly motivated pupils.

The Russian junior art schools of the 1980s provided an interesting if controversial model for solving the problem of how to teach the exceptional and other young people in art. Selected children attended their regular schools during the day but went on to the junior specialist art school in mid-afternoon each day. They were admitted at any timely age (for them) between seven and fourteen years, provided they were eager and showed impressive work. Once admitted, total commitment was expected of students, however young; their studies were strongly organized. But the teaching, by established artists, was remarkably sensitive to the natural thinking of childhood, avoiding the imposition of any prematurely adult or corporate style. Unlike in the academies, there was no imposed hierarchy of learning, but rather a gradual introduction of experiences of new processes, techniques and materials: printmaking and ceramics as well as painting and drawing. Students were accountable not only to tutors but to the community, through a responsibility to display work publicly.[20]

Unlike the academies, the state junior art schools in Russia assumed that only some of their students would eventually become artists, the remainder making an equal but differently useful contribution to the aesthetic and artistic development of community life. But those schools provided a powerful route to artistic professionalism for their most able students, regardless of the expense or their background.

The link between exclusive provision for intending future artists and one which trains the artists alongside others who will make different contributions to society through art, is one variously represented in different countries. In São Paulo, Brazil, where the economy and the educational system are both volatile, determined parents have queued overnight to enter their children in a (city-funded) primary school for tuition in the arts, with ultimate professional roles in music or the visual arts envisaged for their children.

Finland, on the other hand, set up new government-authorized part-time art schools for children in the late 1970s, in which children from the age of five up to eighteen years can receive art training. The curriculum and the teaching are kept as flexible as possible in order to provide a general artistic education as well as to accommodate the training of future artists.[21] The dual purpose of such courses has the advantage of giving future artists a broader base for their cultural experience and development; it is arguable whether it also leads in practice to a dilution of teaching and provision.

Attitudes in the United States, while understandably different among individual states, tend to favour the idea of provision of separate training for those exhibiting high performance 'and who, by reason thereof, require services or activities not ordinarily provided' by the general system. This statement, from a report made to the United States Congress in 1972,[22] also heralded a new national policy on the 'gifted and talented' which resulted in the establishment of supportive networks and some financial provision.

The real outcomes from this initiative seem to have been patchy and disappointing. Twelve years after the report, only ten of the states were claiming to have initiated programmes of visual art training for exceptional students and only one state (California) could produce a specific policy statement for such provision.[23] The integrated rather than the separated high-ability programmes in art seem to have been somewhat easier to implement. Separated art programmes for the exceptional, where they exist, seem to have imposed rigid entry requirements, focusing so heavily on general intellectual skills (measured, perhaps unwisely, by formal intelligence and achievement tests) that many otherwise exceptional children have been excluded from being considered for them. The focus of the teaching in them seems paradoxically less traditional than the entry requirements suggest (and than is still the case in many similar European courses): both tests and assignments emphasize visual expression, visual memory and originality more than processes, techniques and historical subject-matter.

In Britain in the 1920s, a number of dedicated junior art-training establishments were founded which admitted pupils from around eleven years of age. Their purpose was initially more to generate a new breed of designers for industry than to plug the gap in the training of artists between the loss of opportunity for early entry to the academies and the bland art provision of the state school system. But, although the needs of industry were well served, the new schools proved a godsend to eager but frustrated young individuals who wished to begin their training as artists; 'I wanted to go to that school [Derby Junior Art Department] ever since I was five and drawing at the kitchen table', recalled Margaret Hine; she went at eleven, later becoming a distinguished ceramic artist and painter in England in the 1960s.[24] Many went on to senior art schools and to the Royal College of Art, maturing as successful professionals and becoming influential for many years as art tutors at all educational levels.

These schools were in fact mostly junior departments of senior art schools, with a broad subject curriculum, but giving nearly as much time to the study and practice of art as to the study of the other subjects jointly. During the forty years of their existence, they were the only available source of early art training in the country, apart from one or two private art schools for those who could afford them. The focus of the teaching was on drawing of a fairly traditional approach, involving the study of form, tone and geometry, and applied to lettering, design, modelling and commercial art, with selected craft work according to local strengths. It was intended to prepare students for relatively modest employment in industry. Admission criteria implied that a high potential in art compensated for an assumed lower academic ability, unlike in the more recent American model. Students who were more intelligent astutely concealed that ability on entry, grasping the best aspects of the art tuition, evading entrapment into lesser employment and pursuing their future as artists.

For reasons economic and political as well as broadly educational, the eventual forty such junior art schools were all victims of change in Britain in the 1960s and 70s. The idea of specialist art secondary schools that were proposed to replace them barely surfaced long enough to be cancelled. One such school in Manchester lasted for only a few years, even though it was highly regarded during its lifetime under the inspired guidance of Ernest Goodman. Finances and premises were soon reallocated to feed the burgeoning undergraduate art education system, with the entry barrier raised, not just to sixteen but to eighteen years all round. Few of those who passed through the junior departments so eagerly and successfully and who became influential as artists and teachers are now young enough to continue in those roles. Unlike Finland, the Russian centres and some countries in the Americas, Britain no longer has such early training opportunities, even though junior schools specializing in training for the professions of music, dance, drama and sport are on the increase. Early training in art is still in abeyance.

Definition, quality and rights

All these differences of attitude and provision between countries, fluctuating over time in any one of them, reflect the confusions which have always existed about artists and about the process of becoming an artist. We are unsure what it actually means to be an artist – whether it is a profession, an inherited or acquired condition, a blessing, a talent or even a malady. And because art itself is so differently viewed at the present time, it is even more difficult to resolve issues of quality about artists and what they create.

In particular, the vision of a society in which some who may not become professional artists can nevertheless be aided to make an important contribution to its aesthetic achievements is a rare phenomenon. Any idea of the right of *all* individuals to visual expressive fluency is as yet hardly recognized.

2

Characteristics of the developing artist

As I sieved my past I found that the seeds of all that obsesses me in my art and life were sown much earlier than I had guessed.

Tom Phillips, *Works and Texts* (1992)

To be or to become an artist?

Are there any definable differences between those young individuals who eventually become artists and their peers who do not? Do the former possess from the very beginning an exceptional sensitivity towards all things visual, an urge to imagine and to originate, an impulse to record and to express? Are they in some way selected for such a future before they have vacated the womb and gulped their first breaths of air? If the answers to these questions are in the affirmative, it would mean that most people must regard themselves as genetically ineligible for the role, no matter how appropriate an education and training they might undergo.

It is a popular view that certain rare individuals are born with highly exceptional ability in at least one respect; you have it or you do not. The description usually applied to them, that they are 'gifted', rarely has a religious meaning nowadays. It is used, as the English writer Alan Bennett laments, to imply effort-less and almost unfair facility which ought therefore somehow to incur a debt: 'We call it a gift, but some-how, somewhere, we expect it to be paid for, by poverty, or deprivation or unhappiness'.[1] The 'gift' itself, and not just its image, is sometimes viewed as a burden by those who think they have it; another writer, Rumer Godden, suggested that 'It is not a gift you can ignore – it demands your attention and you have to design the rest of your life to live with it'.[2]

Some artists feel that the 'gift' renders them different from the very beginning from other people. At the most extreme they may, like the Spanish Surrealist painter Salvador Dali, have identified their exception-ality with genius; for such an individual, wrote Dali, 'his sleep, his digestion, his ecstasies, his nails, his colds, his blood, his life and death are essentially different from those of the rest of mankind'.[3] But extreme instances tend to be the most visible, and the alleged difference from others may be more a strong variation. A second Dali is indeed unlikely, but art shows us that aspects of his personality or his artistic achievements may well be echoed in the work of others. And Dali's view of himself sets him and, by implication, all significant art and major artists un-comfortably apart from their culture and society.

Another and earlier Spanish artist, Goya, looked for evidence of his own genius less mystically and more logically in his art rather than in his being. His 'discovery' that it only became apparent to himself if he 'dared to *give up aiming to please*'[4] defines the exceptional or the genius-artist by the idiosyncratic nature of the endeavour. Bernhard Berenson's view is similar but more explicit; genius for him is 'the capacity for productive reaction against one's train-ing',[5] emphasizing an important responsive and even rebellious aspect of the phenomenon, which is not just about being special but unconventional.

The evidence is slightly more persuasive for some kind of inherited facility which favours (even if it does not guarantee) becoming an artist than for the total uniqueness of a few individuals. In some families, several generations of artists emerge. But there is no consistent view on this; Jon Stallworthy notes, for instance, that 'it is surprising how few notable poets have poets for parents or children'.[6] Among an artist's several children, perhaps only one (if any) may pursue the parental interests, while others of the same family do not. In some families of professional artists there is even evidence of a wish to avoid becoming an artist, presumably because of a feeling – quite natural in adolescence – of wanting to separate from parental influence. Sometimes the initial urge to adopt the same profession is daunted by a glowing image of parental achievement; the sculptor Henry Moore's daughter Mary is said to have made her first entry to the Slade School's life room furtively, hoping to conceal her identity.

But artist-children of artist-parents are certainly not uncommon. The example of someone working as an artist is there to inspire and intrigue, the materials are temptingly available, the advice is probably on offer. Surrounded by relatives who painted, the young Toulouse-Lautrec (see below, Chapter 4) must have seen drawing and painting as natural activities for his aristocratic family, even if not for the household staff. The English painter Sarah Raphael (discussed in Chapter 8, below) comments that one of her daughters draws obsessively, adopting the same physical strategies of looking intensely and alternately at subject and paper as she has seen her mother employ.

Nevertheless the existence of even a few families with a sustained artistic lineage may have some genetic as well as social significance. Individuals do appear to behave differently from birth (or even just prior to it); infants do appear to act individually, to be more or less energetic, perceptive, knowing and imaginative. It is hardly surprising that the organism we know as human, most favoured by Nature when not inbred, should display such early physical and psychological differences, unlikely all to have been learned in a brief period following birth. It is surprising that so much research has focused on the pursuit of the concept of a common innate inheritance, rather than on a varied inheritance and its interaction with personal experience.

Differences of inheritance between individuals could account for the different enthusiasms we all display and to an extent the different levels of confidence and ability which are variable and apparent between us. But such dispositions do not seem in themselves to guarantee particular developments. Some seem to be strengthened by experience, others are weakened by it. And it is not just in the things that we feel ill-equipped to do that we may fail to flourish; it is sometimes also in those capacities that seem promising. So it is at least possible that a disposition to be 'artistic' (however that may eventually be defined) is present in more individuals than those who actually show it, and that the manifestation of exceptional skills in art is conditional, if not always wholly dependent, upon the circumstances of childhood.

Some artists less egocentric than Dali do see the impetus for their work as having emerged from the social or psychological circumstances of their lives rather than from some innate disposition as such. The composer Aaron Copeland explained that 'I must create in order to know myself'.[7] The painter Stanley Spencer advanced a more compensatory view: 'My desire to paint is caused by my being unable – or incapable – of fulfilling my desires in life itself'. These are, of course, hindsight explanations; many of those who recall their first reasons for choosing to study visual art will say that they simply (and passionately) wanted to draw and rarely add that they had any particular projected purpose for the skill of drawing; it was felt to be a rewarding, not to say heady and demanding, experience in its own right and without the need for, or possibility of, explanation. That apparently simple preoccupation may have been the only outward evidence at the time of a tendency to be artistic. Curiously, it only sometimes indicates the kind of imaginative approach to the making of images that one might expect to see in a future artist.

Though quite common for an eventually successful artist, an early start does not seem to be essential. Late-developing artists seem to emerge when careers initially chosen or lifestyles imposed by circumstance prove unsatisfactory. For those others to whom this late start nowadays happens as a diversion in retirement, it remains a matter of simple crafting of images in the manner of others; it is enough to behave like an artist rather than actually to become one; the motivation is entertainment, rarely passion. For a few late-starters, the outcomes are spectacular, often powerful individualistic achievements and, like Gauguin's, little conditioned by formal art training. Such artists appear to be impelled by a previously pent-up force as well as guided somehow by newly formed instincts towards original expression.

The so-called 'primitive' artist Alfred Wallis began to paint only in his seventies, after the death of his wife in 1922 and, as he himself put it, 'for company' (see pl.1). Once he had started, he worked with an intensity which fascinated those who saw it; he 'used to be forever painting … nothing was safe from where paint could go, like', as a contemporary witness recalled.[8] Sven Berlin, in his book about that tormented but exceptional artist, suggests that:

Had Wallis's life been different from the beginning, had it not, even apart from the economic problem, been so extraordinarily involved with tragedy and disappointment, had it, in fact, been normal, it is most certain that he would never have painted, or been, in himself, the dramatic personality he was. Right education, cultural, economic and religious environment … Had those things been his, he would have been a happy, integrated human being … and his natural creative capacities would have flowed into all the avenues and alleyways of daily life.

Berlin adds his belief that 'the only difference between child and mature artist is that the latter has as his heritage, the arts of all time and the experience of complex development'.[9]

Berlin's main contention is that the circumstances, more than the individual, bring about development as an artist. He attributes both the torment and the art to much earlier and longer-term circumstances than those identified by Wallis himself. It is possible that the building up of emotional pressures from the working and domestic lives of such individuals creates the inner drive which eventually generates fierce endeavour; the work emerges as a kind of liberating force from the earlier and perhaps frustrating experiences. The question remains as to whether *any* such individual might respond in this way or whether Wallis had carried with him from childhood, or even before, some particular disposition which caused him eventually to respond as he did.

There are numerous apparent examples of the 'trauma-to-creative-obsession' view which Berlin espouses. Some of the most interesting describe the powerful changes effected in the nature of artistic activity in particular individuals who were already artists. Goya suffered a highly traumatic physical and mental illness in mid-career, possibly with psychological as well as physical causes. Harold Osborne records that, although 'his artistic activity remained unaffected … signs of emotional change became apparent'.[10] This is both inaccurate and understated; the cloying compliance of the hired painter which characterizes much of Goya's work prior to his illness is subsequently replaced by a potent and frightening energy, expressive of a very different artist. The paintings and etchings he then produced are often darkly menacing, brutally explicit, critically realistic or savagely satirical.

Another account, of the tragically brief life of the First World War poet Wilfred Owen, sees his last and greatest poems not only as an extension of his earlier work but as a direct and powerful outcome of his close encounter with the monstrous horror of war. John Ezard describes how the influence of his fellow psychiatric patient Siegfried Sassoon gave Owen new creative energy: 'the stress that poured from him was shaped into work of quality which fulfilled all his years of experimentation with technique'. Owen himself described the sense of renewal and release which he felt: 'I go out of this year a poet … as which I did not enter it … I am started. The tugs have left me; I feel the great swelling of the open sea taking my galleon.'[11] Owen went on to write ten of the most remarkable poems lamenting war before becoming a victim of it himself.

These fascinating examples of the relationship between an individual's circumstances and their consequences for the stimulation of creative energy and action may reasonably be applied to the situation of the child. They do not in themselves preclude the possibility that such individuals, whether in childhood or maturity, possess innate qualities which make development as an artist more likely and perhaps actually possible.

A disposition for development

It is strange to argue that artists are always those for whom life is hellish and that contented, rounded individuals do little that is creative, even if Freud concluded so after studying too many neurotics. More recent attempts to analyse sources of creative energy have focused on the consequences, not so much of external pressures as of inner psychological ones, investigating individuals who present themselves as neurotic patients, perhaps more inherently neurotic than the specifically war-damaged Owen.

One such study, by the psychologist John Gedo in 1972, was of a patient judged to be exceptionally creative to the point of genius. This individual had allegedly developed, early in life, 'conflict-free autonomous [creative] capacities'.[12] Gedo imagines the likely childhood of the subject in such a way as to suggest a person of ordinary capabilities in most things but with some exceptional abilities 'beyond those of ordinary mortals'; the implication of immortality is intriguing. From childhood the patient had felt himself to be both quite ordinary and in some respects also extraordinary, 'like a cuckoo in a nest of sparrows', as Gedo suggests. Maturing, he passed through stages of grandiosity and disillusionment, searching always to replace the fallible with the idealizable in the family and in religion and finally finding it in his own creative work, a description suggesting Gedo's own unawareness of the alarming uncertainty experienced continually by most practising artists.

Gedo argues that his patient could only avoid 'the threat of a deficit in his self-esteem' by continually and relentlessly regenerating the creative act. His explanation for the creative disposition is that it is an emergent consequence of and defence against emotional instability. He accepts that this is evidence derived from only one example, but argues that the lives of three eminent individuals – Freud, Leonardo and Goethe – provide generally similar evidence. One can only remain unsurprised that the study of neurotic patients throws up descriptions of high trauma, with creative action cast in the therapy role as well as being trauma-induced. Such explanations seem entirely valid for some individuals, but inadequate for the entire range of the creative impulse and artistic obsession.

And no explanation is offered for the earlier development of those creative capacities which became evident to Gedo in his patient in connection with later psychological phenomena.

A predisposition that would make artistic activity and the passion for it more likely, present from the beginning and not dependent for its existence solely upon accident or trauma, seems a notion reinforced rather than invalidated by this account; Gedo's patient displayed creative interests *before* his psychological problems were evident. But such a phenomenon may indeed occur as just one extraordinary aspect of an otherwise apparently normal individual, as Gedo proposes, or even of an apparently otherwise limited person; it is said of the composer Richard Wagner that his early promise was signalled by the absence of some of the many skills common to others which he did not exhibit. Alternatively the drive to create may be matched by other exceptional interacting capacities and skills.

That alternative matches what we know of Leonardo da Vinci, the polymath – an engineer and designer as well as a visual artist, rather than of J. M. W. Turner, for example, who only displayed exceptional skills as a painter. However, Turner's important innovations in landscape painting might be adjudged more the work of a genius than might the paintings of a polymath. An element of personal courage is involved too; both child and adult need determination to overcome the feelings of insecurity inherent in the expressive act.

The powerful obsession and the intensity of action so often evident in the late-developing artist are also characteristic of the early developer, as Vasari noted in his *Lives of the Artists*. He records how the painter Fra Filippo Lippi as a child 'spent all his time scrawling pictures on his own books and those of others'; that the child Leonardo 'never ceased drawing' and that the young Raphael was 'so obsessed by drawing that he used to spend on it all the time he could'.[13]

There is no shortage of more recent descriptions of this phenomenon. The Swiss painter Paul Klee, a child in the nineteenth century and a mature artist mainly in the twentieth, is said as a child to have drawn constantly 'whatever came into his head' and often to have done so using both hands,[14] as though in too much of a hurry perhaps to wait for the achievements of only one (see fig.2.1). The Welsh painter Kyffin Williams even asserts that all he had in the beginning was an obsession with drawing, without any apparent facility as such.[15] It is the intensity of the impulse described in such examples of early obsessive drawing activity, often pursued against discouragement, which seems to suggest a genetic disposition of some kind. Nothing else can quite explain the power of the obsession or its

2.1 Paul Klee, *Woman and child*, c.1889 (age 10)

persistence in specific cases. Without such a disposition and this apparent manifestation of it, all the other circumstances might possibly still be enough to facilitate a satisfactory life as an artist. With it, the opportunities so fiercely and impatiently seized upon may prove essential for accelerative development and (ultimately) the very highest achievement.

Even in those so dynamically empowered, it seems that the disposition to draw can be substantially affected by circumstance. Repression as an impediment to development is self-evident in innumerable instances in childhood and adolescence, as it is in mature life, in the obvious reduction of achievement. Such a reduction is often viewed as inevitable, rather than as a consequence of adverse circumstances which, had they been different, might have sustained the creative energy initially present.

Families and their influence

Where attention has centred on the circumstances which might be thought to encourage the development of artistic fluency in the young, independently of any assumption of prior disposition, the family environment has been identified (unsurprisingly) as important. The attitudes of families appear to be crucially formative on children who are aesthetically and artistically outstanding,[16] attitudes which are implicit in the provision of space, materials, time, privacy, contact with art and interesting people and all the other manifestations of support and encouragement.

Could such apparently ideal circumstances for development ever be sufficient in themselves? The father of the nineteenth-century English painter W. P. Frith provided immense practical encouragement in advancing his son towards what eventually became a distinguished artistic career. In his autobiography, Frith describes how his father keenly promoted his artistic training when he himself did not feel particularly motivated and only cooperated in deference to his father's wishes.[17] If these recollections are accurate, Frith seems, unusually, to have become an artist without the urge to do so.

The role of a parent (or parent-figure) in the nourishing of artistic activity has an honourable history, at least in the case of male children. It is difficult not to mention the child prodigy Mozart, who performed at the piano, again to please his father; by the age of six, he displayed his incredibly developed musical skills on a European concert tour – he could, for instance, identify all the musical intervals produced by the random striking of glasses, clocks, cups and saucers. Rebellious though he may have been, his father's influence was strong upon him and he seems to have soaked up experience like a sponge. Certainly Picasso began to draw at least in part to attract his father's attention, even if his paramount objective later was to remove himself from parental dominance (see Chapter 5).

Escaping from the family ambience is a recurrent theme in the lives of artists, although the reasons differ. In the case of Klee, it has been argued, for instance, that 'Heredity, upbringing and his own personality made an artist of Klee. In his case his need to escape was merely an extension of his personality and not an expression of revolt against the milieu in which he lived, as it was in the case of many other artists.' His relationship with his father was positive, as letters to him (in which he confides his artistic ambitions) show.[18]

The preservation of a child's drawings, when it happens, has often been done by the mother, and the maternal parent can often be identified as having been a benevolent but usually less interventional observer. Keeping such drawings is at least an indulgent action; at most it denotes a positive judgement on the activity and its achievements, sometimes with an element of selection if not censorship.

The enthusiasm and supportive indulgence of parents may go very wrong. Of Maria del Rosario, Goya's pupil and possibly his daughter, it is said that this talented child was extensively overtaught by him,

so that after his death she was unable to do more than echo his achievement.[19] The first eighteen years of the development of 'Peter' (a pseudonym for an individual whose case I have studied) provide a recent example of the same problem. At six, he exhibited exceptional artistic energy and skill; his drawings from the years between six and twelve, although somewhat marred by a parental emphasis on copying and overblown still-life studies, still show his feeling for observation and for recreating experience. But by twelve years the parents' intensive drive to get him to perform as an artist, rather than to *develop* as one, had taken its toll; a self-image as a genius had been thrust upon him to such an extent that he was unable to relate well to other children beyond the family. The consequent trauma of unhappy schooling and an instilled distrust even of good teachers caused him to reject tuition and gradually to spurn the very activity at which he had excelled.

Even when the family environment is not positively damaging in this way, it can sometimes be so aesthetically and artistically barren as to discourage all but the most determined future artist. Lucky is the artistic child like the young Michael Rothenstein, growing up among the stimuli of art objects, books and the lively conversation of distinguished family visitors. By contrast, the painter Tom Phillips recalls a family home devoid of pictures: 'My father's photo on the mantlepiece between two Chinese vases did suggest a world of imagery just out of reach' (see pl.II), and another British artist, Howard Hodgkin, remembers the total irrelevance of art to life in his family home, even though by the age of five he somehow knew he had decided to become an artist.[20] From such a visual and intellectual vacuum it must have been a struggle to emerge, imagine and create. On the positive side, Phillips' account hints at his childhood capacity to imagine what might be, even from such limited and stultifying experience.

Whatever the practical facilities and support provided in the family home, it is not always the case that they extend to the provision of adequate mental space for creative thinking and working; some domestic situations can be claustrophobic. Whether recognized, as in Paula Rego's appraisal of a childhood like her own, 'where you are stuck in a room all day', as 'the best training for a painter', or implicit, as in Vasari's account of Giotto's opportunity, as a shepherd boy, to carve on stones, space and time may be even more important than more tangible forms of support.

Chance circumstances can provide the ideal generative situation; the English painter Paul Nash obtained space for his artistic development because of the absence during his childhood of his mother, through illness.[21] Much has been written about the necessity of solitude for and of the artist – 'Conversation enriches understanding but solitude is the school of genius', according to Edward Gibbon – but there has been confusion between notions of the artist as essentially reclusive or as simply in need of working-time away from others.

To go in search of lonely children in order to find creative ones would hardly be justified, even though the creative may sometimes be lonely. The illustrator Beatrix Potter, prolific in drawing as a child, was physically isolated rather like the young Paula Rego, but in her case as a consequence of Victorian middle-class attitudes to children: kept safe and apart from adults at home, she was taught separately without the stimulus of peers.[22] But the Anglo-Russian ballet dancer Rudolf Nureyev, although educated in a school, found that he was lonely because he was ostracized by other pupils, since he could do things they could not.

The artistically motivated child sometimes has to make a choice, either to pursue creative ambition without regard for its social consequences or to conceal it in order to seem more like others. At home the obsession may continue unimpeded, although the extent to which its manifestations are shared with the family may depend upon the nature of their support more than on any need for detachment. Solitude is possibly more a practical requirement of the creative process than an essential characteristic of a creative person; many artists are gregarious people when not at work.

Adult mentors play a major part in shaping a child's own self-image, which is a crucial factor for the future of all children but particularly for creative individuals. A vision of the possible and of one's own potential for innovation underpins creative action; without that particular sense of self, innate and learned capacities may not be fully exploited. In some societies and some epochs, the concept of the creative child and of its extreme, the *wunderkind* or prodigy, is more welcome than in others. But to be caused to feel very different from others can be detrimental. 'Peter's' image of himself was imposed by others and he appeared unnerved by it.[23]

Some determined children seem able to see themselves as artists against the vision of their parents, but if this is the case, there is usually some other supportive influence. The British sculptor Rebecca Horn observes:

'As a little girl, my parents were always worried what I would come up with next. I was an only child and I was brought up to be independent, I had a marvellous Romanian governess who taught me to draw before I went to school. I was the only one in my class who could draw when I was five, and they made a big fuss of me; I was a star. I decided to be an artist then, although my parents said, no, no, girls don't become artists.'[24]

Education in art

Education begins informally at home. When a child shows early facility in art in a supportive family, that support is likely to determine not only the materials used and the scale of the earliest work, but also subject-matter and style. Adult artistic preferences inevitably infuse the assistance received. The grandmother of Paul Klee and the mother of Gerard Hoffnung clearly favoured religious themes (see Chapter 7); the child John Ruskin absorbed a detailed classical drawing style.[25] In families where a professional eye is lacking, the preferred image of art can sometimes cloy or inhibit unless parents are open to a child's perceptions. Available cases suggest that these earliest experiences are deeply formative with the absorption of much influence, even where exceptional ability causes more independent developments.

The first experience of formal education for any child may generate tension between teacher and pupil which is less evident inside the family. Stronger children may react against teaching by ignoring advice, or may draw with obliging convention at school while doing their most individual work at home. This autonomous attitude seems to be a possible indicator of artistic commitment. Creative flexibility, so important to the development of an artist, may begin here in this tendency to evasion.

In contemporary education, the teaching of specific skills of drawing and art prior to adolescence (and sometimes beyond it) has been regarded by some as interference with otherwise natural processes. Sven Berlin was one of many who argued that the child's natural manner of painting is 'both faultless and adequate'.[26] A consequence of such 'interference' that is commonly evident is a rapid adoption of the social conventions of drawing, as the only available proto-types. Others have claimed that constructive teaching *of some kind* at this early stage is crucial to long-term achievement.

This important issue is about the relevance of any teaching at all and at any stage to artistically exceptional individuals. We cannot, for instance, judge whether those individuals who became artists only in maturity could have benefited from it (Berlin thinks not). Some would say that they lacked necessary representational skills and acquaintance with enough examples of expressive techniques; others might argue that these could well have damaged the free approach which lies at the heart of their ultimate achievements. Edwin Mullins notes that Wallis's technique was

1 Alfred Wallis, *Voyage to Labrador*, 1932–42

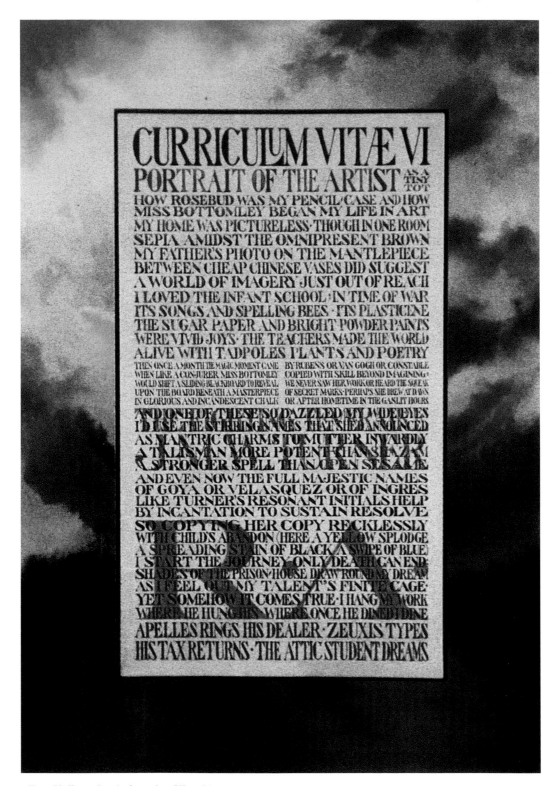

II Tom Phillips, *Curriculum vitae VI*, 1986

III John Everett Millais, *Study of a rock*, 1842 (age 13)

iv Pablo Ruiz Picasso, *Primera Comunión*, 1896 (age 14–15)

v Michael Rothenstein, *Birds on leafy branches*, 1916–17
(age 8–9)

VI Gerard Hoffnung, *Storks at work* (detail), 1932 (age 7)

VII Sarah Raphael, *Strip 5* (detail), 1998

VIII David Downes, *Peregrine falcon*, 1986 (age 15)

'untrained and intuitive' but that, far from being disadvantageous, 'a passionate and adult vision' is effective precisely because it is improvised.[27]

In examples of artists from the nineteenth century, early tutoring is a common phenomenon. Like others at the time, the English Pre-Raphaelite painter John Everett Millais was tutored from the age of four, specifically in formal drawing skills. Tutoring for his family was affordable and parental interest strong; the prospect of an eminent professional future in art was taken seriously and the assumption, true for that time, was that the disciplines and conventions of drawing were an essential and urgent prerequisite for acceptance as a student. But the case for such tuition has changed, partly because art itself has changed – witness the anguish of Picasso in judging his father's tuition as having been too early, too rigorous and too damaging of his natural approach. Consider also the anxieties of the English painter Lucian Freud as a young student; he had felt obliged to resist opportunities for formal training in drawing offered by the eminent teacher Bernard Meninsky: 'I thought that was a threat which I didn't want to give in to'.[28]

In the twentieth century the focus of what is valued in art shifted away from narrative and representation towards the pre-eminence of medium, technique and expression. The preparation of an individual to become an artist (and indeed the induction of everyone into art) has become controversial. Picasso's and Freud's anxieties about formal teaching stemmed from a belief in the repressive consequences associated with traditional teaching methods, in which the assumption has always been that first you learn the historically accepted practical skills and after that you become an artist. There is no evidence that possession of the former guarantees the latter and some infer, with Mullins about Wallis, that such a didactic sequence tends to deflect creative potential.

Throughout some educational systems this debate continues, with students variously experiencing an amalgam of attitudes at different stages and with formal examinations often seriously distorting the experience they have. As future artists develop greater strengths, it may matter less how they are taught than simply that they are enabled to work and encouraged to do so. The painter Sarah Raphael describes how (in adolescence) the discovery of an art teacher who would simply leave her alone to work was a helpful experience (see Chapter 8). But even the strong may suffer from lack of suitable support at the right moment.

The pianist Mark Hambourg puts a musician's view of unsatisfactory teaching in a psychological context. He refers to Karl Popper's proposition that there are three worlds of human experience: the first physical world, the second psychological world of human potentialities and dimensions and the third arena of culture, ideas, artefacts, theories and creations. He argues that 'Giftedness is an event in World Two … Without its rebirth into World Three, without transformation into cultural achievement, it is of no more value than the gleam of Narcissus in the pool'.[29] He laments the fact that excellent technical expertise is often presented as an achievement in its own right without the development of interpretation and expression. He describes some 'gifted' children as being bored and refusing to continue because they have attained technical expertise to a high level but have not been shown how it relates to their own world.

Given the pressures and the pitfalls for anyone of growing up, it would hardly be surprising if there are many more young individuals with exceptional artistic ability than eventually mature as artists. For many, as another celebrated pianist, Artur Schnabel, once cynically remarked, 'the Wunder goes but the Kind remains'.[30] One may never know whether any successful artists could have been prevented from becoming so by bad or absent teaching. We do know from Vasari of medieval and Renaissance artists whose early years were a struggle, not just against the inadvertently discouraging but against active discouragement. Raphael was, as we have seen, obsessed by drawing in spite of being beaten by his father and other members of his family, according to Vasari, but this is an example from the highest level of exceptionality. Others may be more easily deflected, where sensitive teaching might otherwise avoid wasting their potential.

Personality and attitudes

Exceptional young individuals generally are frequently described as exhibiting:

- high intelligence and the ability to analyse and to abstract
- rapid learning skills and unusually retentive memory
- exceptional curiosity and tenacity
- a tireless imagination
- unusual insightfulness
- an independent if not actually solitary nature.

To this list, and obviously deemed to have been generated by these positive characteristics, can be easily added particular knowledge and abilities in one or more areas of human endeavour, and on the debit side often impatience, unco-operativeness or laziness (in some situations) and a low boredom threshold in specific topic areas.

We can match this list to descriptions of the personalities of specific highly exceptional individuals, where the behaviours are obvious because extreme, and most of it seems justifiable. Bertrand Russell described the philosopher Wittgenstein as 'perhaps the most perfect example I have ever known of genius as traditionally conceived, passionate, profound, intense, and dominating. He had a kind of purity ... his life was turbulent and troubled, and his personal force was extraordinary.'[31]

Another claim might be made for the artistically exceptional, that they must possess singular courage. The international conductor-musician André Previn described in a radio interview how he left a comfortable post as a film musical director, realising that 'It didn't scare me. In order to do good work, you have to be afraid of it.' He therefore sought a challenging independent career, more traumatically creative. But do such individuals actually have the choice which courage implies? Joshua Bell, a violin virtuoso prodigy, was described by his father as withdrawing into a trance-like state of total absorption, not just when playing the violin but when competing at games or using a computer, capable of excluding all else to such an extent that his 'gift' was extremely destructive in the family.[32] This sounds less like courage or even ruthlessness, much more like uncontrollable obsession.

Tenacity is also significant in the longer term. Much is written about what Sven Berlin called 'the turning away from the imaginative world at around seven or eight years', induced, he argued, by 'the prejudices of society'.[33] Perhaps the phenomenon he describes occurs later than he has suggested and it may be that the remarkable early flexibility displayed by many exceptional children helps them to resist its effects. If so, it may be possible to prepare others similarly to counter them.

Many of the traits I have itemized can be found represented to the same or lesser degrees in all kinds of creative professionals, whether in the arts or the sciences. Of particular interest is the capacity for remembering; exceptional memory skills are often linked with exceptional creative skills, enabling sustained and accurate retention from incredibly rapid intake of images or ideas. As a child, David Downes (see Chapter 9) could absorb details of architecture or of paintings in a gallery without even appearing to look directly at them.

The list remains contentious, most importantly in its reference to high intelligence. Artistic skills in particular have long been argued not to be intelligence-dependent; the historical view lingers on of the artist as mere artisan. And in education art has been commonly designated a 'non-academic' part of the curriculum, even to the point of arguing that it is a subject for those who find the academic too difficult. This is a confusion exacerbated by mistaking the leisure mode of art activity for its serious disciplined study. Far from being solely practical, the latter requires the student to inform and imbue the practical with a growing awareness of its philosophical, symbolic and imaginative aspects as well as those which are visual and practical. Such demands render the study of art as much 'academic' as the study of, say, history or mathematics, with all the requirements of intelligent, abstract thinking that the term usually implies.

This confusion has not prevented many from seeking evidence of intelligence in art at different developmental stages of the young artist, through prevailing notions of artistic intention and competence. But how important in those terms is it to consider particular practical skills in drawing: dexterity with the tools and materials or being able to reproduce what you see? Are expression, aesthetic sensitivity and imagination as significant to intelligence as they are to art? Some research has focused on the full range of artistic skills beyond the practical, on skills of interpretation as well as practical performance. When it has, the role of intelligence in the aesthetic and the imaginative has been more obvious.[34] Too often, investigating intelligence through the arts rather than through visual art has confused the issues too; the skills of aesthetic interpretation in music, for example, may be parallel to those in art but the performance skills have very different criteria. Paul Klee noted that in childhood he chose to become a visual artist rather than a musician because he perceived the former to offer 'the possibility of truly personal expression', thinking no doubt of the musician as performer rather than as composer.[35]

A major challenge to the notion of art as academic and practical emerges from cases of individuals with exceptional and early skills in drawing who appear to be of impaired intelligence. 'Nadia', an autistic child, drew feverishly though intermittently from infancy.[36] By the age of three, she seemed to know things about 'perspective' drawing of forms in space which some people never assimilate. Her drawings showed horses and riders galloping towards the viewer. Her open-beaked cockerel sketches recreated three dimensions in two. Yet her ability to speak remained limited and her general understanding slight. Perhaps her lack of understanding of her observations meant that she had no concepts to get in the way of her memories of what she saw; her horses and cockerels were nothing more than moving shapes remembered from her field of vision (she rarely drew anything that had not been moving).

Nadia's case raises the question of whether her skill

was fundamentally the same as that shown by others displaying exceptional drawing skills and especially whether high intelligence is in fact an essential constituent for higher artistic performance. In first commenting upon a similar case, that of Stephen Wiltshire, an autistic boy who drew superbly detailed architectural studies from an early age, Sir Hugh Casson rashly pronounced him 'possibly the best child artist in Britain'.[37] Oliver Sacks initially considered him as possibly 'an artist through and through' because while most of his drawings are detailed and well-remembered, he was also capable of the expression of 'pure joy, playfulness, aesthetic delight, art'.[38] But later he perceived the constraints of personality and aptitude which would inhibit Stephen's development as an artist.

Opinion is, thus, divided as to his capability and future. It may well be that such children have a concealed 'intelligence' of a special kind; certain types of autism such as 'Asperger's Syndrome' are more strongly associated with exceptional (though narrow) expressive skills than they are with deficiencies;[39] autism has many forms and only some of them seem to permit positive development. But if some facility is there in an autistic child, it is rarely of a kind sufficient (or accessible enough) for becoming an artist; Stephen's drawings achieved sophistication as detailed evocations of intense recent memories. But, as Boris Ford says in a critique of a book on Stephen's work, it needs to 'become charged with moral and human depth'[40] before it can take on the true dimensions of art[40] and, for Sacks, that will depend on 'how much [Stephen] can develop as a genuine human being, despite being (as he will always be) an autistic person'.

The requisite skills for development as an artist do seem to be strongly linked with personality and autism does appear to inhibit the kind of intelligent awareness which is necessary for its effective growth. Freeman's research discovery that most children with a fine-art disposition 'had the broadest cultural and intellectual interests of all the groups studied and took their aesthetic support from both home and school'[41] supports this view, for development as a person is inevitably a response to social and cultural experience.

It is possible that children who are strongly disposed towards activity in the visual arts have (or rapidly acquire) a particular kind of intelligence that is more visually oriented than may be true of other individuals. Vision and touch are paramount in infancy, becoming less so as new knowledge and more abstract understanding begin to dominate sensory experience; expectation begins to override seeing. Some may be able to sustain visual and tactile dominance, continuing to treat every new experience as novel rather than as confirmation of what is already assumed or understood. This 'innocent eye' is after all what characterizes the vision of the finer visual artist, who focuses strongly on qualities and relationships even when the literal meanings are important too. It is also what many mature artists have tried to recapture, in attempts to penetrate the dense undergrowth of their lifelong cultural development.

Fine art in the twentieth century innovatively emphasized form and expression over and beyond description. In 'About Art and Artistic Talent' Pinchas Noy implicitly endorses that view in arguing the essential difference in the artist from others is 'an especially strong psychological attachment to the primary means of communication which deals more with feelings than meanings',[42] citing Dylan Thomas as an artist clearly conscious of this particular priority in his own approach to writing. The poet did indeed explicitly refer to this himself:

I wanted to write poetry in the beginning because I had fallen in love with words. The first poems I knew were nursery rhymes and before I could read them myself I had come to love just the words of them, the words alone, what the words stood for or symbolised or meant, was of very secondary importance, what mattered was the sound of them as I heard them for the first time on the lips of the remote and incomprehensible grown-ups who seemed for some reason to be living in my world. And these words were, to me, as the notes of bells, the sounds of musical instruments, the noises of wind, sea and rain, the rattle of milk-carts, the clopping of hooves on cobbles, the fingering of branches on the window-pane, might be to someone, deaf from birth, who has miraculously found his hearing.[43]

While most individuals quickly develop a secondary stage of response which prioritizes interpretation and symbolization of experience, the theory suggests that the artistically inclined somehow remain alert to sensation and feeling. This is plausible in so far as the making of art is usually practical, involving a medium and tools, committing the artist to direct statement through them via intuitive processes which cannot be independently rationalized or stated. It is also directly pertinent to what we know of the intense sensory interests of the very young, their fascination with the look of things and the sensations they provoke. And it seems that such interests are deeply valued by modern artists; Matisse declared contemporary life 'profane' in that 'we are so used to seeing things that we no longer look at them'.[44]

Noy's theory could account not only for an initial artistic disposition in certain individuals but for the phenomenon of unbidden exceptional drawing activity in the autistic. It might not actually be necessary to possess the capacity for conscious rational thinking in order to make use of certain such dispositions, if some skills can operate (at a basic level) without the apparent understanding of the operator. Even in the case of those who seem to be more aware of the implications of their early drawing, a capacity to suppress the secondary stage of communication (to which Noy refers), sustaining the dominance of the primary stage for as long as possible, is advantageous to artistic intentions. And once one begins to talk of any dispositions as capable of being suppressed or sustained it is not too difficult to argue that, again, what is really being talked about is the nurture in some of capacities which may be inherent, if dormant, in all.

The issue of the creative individual as not merely lonely but also in some way psychologically unusual recurs in contemporary discourse about artists. While the medieval artist was considered no more than a craftsman and the Renaissance artist learned as an apprentice to pursue the conventions of Classicism, their personalities rated less attention than is the case today. Artists generally appear to exhibit much the same personality tendencies and in the same proportions as non-artists: the more eminent are (by definition) more noticeable. The most that can perhaps be argued is for a certain characteristic ruthlessness in most artists, who will generally protect their working opportunities, whether by the device of having an inviolable studio (being independent?), by frequently avoiding social contacts (appearing isolated or lonely?) or by being contemplative (appearing diffident or uncaring?). Stanley Spencer, when painting in Cookham churchyard, would display a sign asking people not to talk to the artist while he was working; but he was quick to hail someone passing by for a little conversation. Monet is well known to have regulated the invitation of visitors to meals at his house strictly according to the ebb and flow of his painting. Anthony Storr notices that 'many creative people appear to nurture their creative talents more carefully than they do their personal relationships'.[45] Creative children too may instinctively withdraw from what is happening in the home to protect what they do, manifested as an evasion of family responsibility, apparent laziness or being 'in a dream'.

Formative events

Being inclined towards artistic activity is one thing; initiating it is another. Anecdotal evidence suggests that it can sometimes be triggered by a single significant and formative event in an individual's early years, just as later experiences – a death for Wallis, a whole war for Owen – seem to have generated passionate expression for them. The importance of these occurrences in childhood is often unnoticed by surrounding adults. The painter Richard Yeomans remembered (in conversation with me) his desire to become an artist as stemming from one childhood encounter in school when Wilhelm Viola (who wrote about the artist-teacher Franz Cizek) visited his classroom and talked briefly to him. Tom Phillips, in his infant school, watched his teacher demonstrating how paints could be mixed and spread. With hindsight he realizes the importance and total rapture of the moment, how avidly he grasped at the first chance to paint:

(here a yellow splodge
a spreading stain of black a swipe of blue)
I start the journey only death can end
(see his *Curriculum vitae VI*, pl.II).

Some accounts seem to describe a reaction against the trigger experience. The sculptor Rebecca Horn sees an adolescent illness as provocative: 'Perhaps I had to make something positive out of the suffering to survive.'[46] Bereavement is sometimes identified as a reactive trigger: Michelangelo's mother died when he was only six years old. No one can say whether he would have been just as motivated or as exceptional without her early death. But numerous examples of the powerfully stimulating effect of bereavement on mature artists encourage the notion; Tennyson mourned a close friend, Mendelssohn a sister who died young.

While such accounts from the memories of established artists are graphic and plausible, there is nothing to confirm that the activation of a dominant artistic function depends upon trigger events. A combination of propitious or challenging circumstances over longer periods may generate or accelerate artistic activity just as effectively if less dramatically; the Welsh sculptor Tony Stevens worked incessantly as a child with Plasticine (see fig.2.2), in a manner in which, on a different scale and with different materials, he has worked ever since. And the apparent 'decision' to become an artist takes place sometimes so early in life that such events are obscure if not irrelevant. Patrick Heron (according to Mel Gooding) was another who 'knew from the age of three that he would become an artist'. Gooding suggests that you can see this in Heron's earliest drawing, in 'the creative deliberateness of the act' in spite of the natural spontaneity of childhood.[47]

The evidence from drawing

Expectations of drawings, and of art generally, produced by exceptional young individuals have tended to be formed more from tradition, theory and prejudice

2.2 Tony Stevens, *Soldiers and their vehicles*, c.1940 (age 10)

than from careful observation and comparison. On the one hand, the early appearance of clear-cut drawing representations in the conventions of the contemporary culture is what alerts adults to artistic potential; this is what impresses us about the drawings of the autistic, after all. On the other hand, the credibility of the discovery is then tempered by notions of what ought to happen (from psychological theory) or how one provokes artistic behaviour (educational and art theory) which colour expectations of the work itself.

Conventional thinking also presupposes a universal route of some kind for the full development of the necessary skills of the artist, whatever those may be assumed to be. Some simply see it as an uncomplicated journey, often in clearly defined stages or 'steps', from 'incompetence' to 'competence'; Lucian Freud talks about his irritation when people described his childhood drawings as 'primitive' when they are, he argues, merely infantile: 'they took an inability for an affectation', he says.[48] Visual realism is commonly seen as the ultimate goal; but a different desirable objective is suggested by Geidion-Welcker's description of the development of the drawings of Paul Klee as a child:

'At first, humbly devoted to tracing the life of the physical world, his lines, as he matures, appear to take on a more independent life of their own.'[49] That description says much about the perception of Klee's place in time, at a point where preparation, even for the more expressive mode of the twentieth century, is still thought of in conventional terms. Yet longitudinal studies of the exceptional reveal considerable diversity of intention and strategy implicit in every phase of development; there are some common phenomena but there is no essential route.

Any attempt to describe the development of drawing in children with strong artistic potential must be necessarily limited by their sheer individuality. A few shared characteristics seem definable and important:

1 The sheer volume of drawing suggests a practical need, in the way that a ship must maintain an impetus in heavy sea to be able to keep control of direction and progress. It is another matter whether that momentum is constant or fluctuating throughout childhood and adolescence; the latter appears more common.

2 Along with much repetition (rehearsal?) of ideas, a

high degree of flexibility to their revelations seems common, expressed in the structure, style, content and meanings of drawings and indicating dynamic combinations of curiosity, memory and imagination. Since there are many kinds of artists, it may not follow that a busy imagination is more characteristic than an eagerness to draw what is there, though it may be relevant to the eventual quality of achievement.

3 A facility seems apparent for exploiting examples, adopting conventions and responding to social preferences, with the possibility that this eclectic attitude conceals the pursuit of more personal styles and interests.

Beyond these tentative descriptions it is difficult to generalize. Even on an apparently simple issue like the degree of dexterity exhibited in manipulating drawing and painting tools, where one might expect to see greater facility and control, there is some contrary evidence that early inhibited manipulative skill sometimes leads to ultimately greater expressive panache in drawing.[50] And little can be said with any confidence about the likely drawing strategies which individuals in general may adopt: the kinds of images they may favour, the pace of their learning, the sources and sustainment of their ideas and the ways they find to express them as they grow older.

These inevitable limitations upon description make the certainty of spotting future excellence as an artist extremely difficult. No one can deny that in some cases it looks as if it could have been predictable, assuming common agreement on the particular phenomena which might signal that excellence. But which phenomena are the best indicators of what sort of future artist? And what if, as is arguably the case for the eminent Spanish artist Joan Miró, there is little evidence in early artistic activity of major promise? Michael Howe's research has indicated that 'by no means all outstanding adults were prodigies as children'.[51] Even so, there is a school of thought which sees mature excellence in art as directly emerging from childhood without any need for an intervening 'apprenticeship'; Gustave Courbet is cited in this respect.[52] And there are now more artists who are aware of the continuity of their own development and even of how little they believe their working processes to have changed over the years. Tom Phillips claims that 'I'm quite childish and I make my work, however sophisticated its terms seem to be, with a childish kind of delight … I still love to make lists and catalogues, build up sets of things, invent codes, form rules and rituals, keep diaries, and to show off in general.'[53]

But the three characteristics tentatively proposed above do offer the beginnings of a description of development. Having been effective for known exceptional individuals, they might be helpful for others, especially if that description can be extended through a deeper investigation of the progress of some specific artists. The seven studies which follow represent a wide spectrum of development as well as showing that some phenomena are shared.

3

Academic training and an independent attitude:
John Everett Millais (1829–1897)

What Luquet, for a later stage of development, calls a
'duplicité de types', is, in my view, present from the beginning ... two different styles of representation: one for [the
child's] own personal satisfaction, the other for other people.

Herbert Read, *Education through Art* (1943)

By the end of the 1820s, when Millais was born in the
South of England, Raphael had been dead for more
than 300 years and the English artist J. M. W. Turner
had been a Royal Academician in London for eighteen
years, having entered the Academy as a student in
1789, at the age of fourteen. Millais was to become a
founder-member of the Pre-Raphaelite Brotherhood,
which (some say arrogantly) challenged the artistic
credibility of Raphael and his school. In childhood he
was also to enter the Royal Academy Schools at an age
younger than Turner and younger than any student
before or since.

Judgements of his eventual position in British
nineteenth-century art are conflicting. The Brotherhood's unorthodox views of the post-Raphael tradition
were initially supported by influential contemporaries,
including the writer and artist John Ruskin, and it is
said that at least one of Millais' major works, *The Order
of Release* (1853), was greatly revered by Delacroix.
Others say that his work, initially exquisitely detailed
and powerful, gradually became superficial and coarse,
that he forsook his challenging theories to become
fashionable and financially successful. An account of
the nineteenth century in British art would, however,
seem inadequate without recognition of the contribution of his major works, ideas and leadership
(within and beyond the Brethren) to that tradition.
Certainly, albeit reactively, English nineteenth-century
painting was modified by the Pre-Raphaelite initiative
and Millais' paintings are still valued as evidence of
that.

A good number of Millais' early drawings have been
preserved, many by his mother, representing in continuous sequence his childhood and adolescence. These
early works reveal obvious skills of draughtsmanship
and reflect the conventions of the period; selected
items have occasionally been exhibited and are regarded as collectors' pieces. Notable among these is
Hebe, a portrait of a racehorse (done at fifteen years)
and a composition, *Brigands Surprised* (done at seventeen years). A framed group of sketches done when he
was seven has also been exhibited. Apart from these
and a few others, little attention had been paid to the
earliest works. Indeed, they were kept in several
different houses until I assembled them chronologically in 1981 for an exhibition (intended primarily
for educationalists) called 'Six Children Draw' at
London University.

Millais was born in Southampton, England, the
youngest of three children. Between four and eight
years of age he lived in the family home on the
Channel Island of Jersey. In a biography of his great-
grandfather, Geoffroy Millais infers that Millais'
interest in drawing did not begin until he was about
four years of age,[1] and there are no drawings in-
disputably associated with the years before he was
six; no work of the more gestural, instinctive and
pre-cultural kind is preserved. We know that he was
expelled from his first (local) school because he was
difficult and uncooperative; his mother taught him for
a while and was thus well placed to observe his facility
at drawing. Since his father was keenly interested in
the arts, a tutor, Mr Bessell, was soon hired to teach
him drawing.

It is possible that the collection includes drawings
Millais made prior to the age of seven. But none record any schematic stage such as most children pass
through today. Progression for him must have been
rapid; by the time of the first identifiable drawings,
at the age of seven, he was already capable of well-
observed, coherent and expressive sketches of horses,

3.1 John Everett Millais, Classical head (copy), 1836 (age 7)

riders and ships, imaginative figure compositions and strongly executed copies of the drawings of others. What part his formal tuition played in these productions is uncertain. This none too amenable pupil (but determined artist) could have initiated the outdoor sketches himself; they are executed with a delicious freedom and simplicity, likely to be less than welcome to his conventional tutor. They seem to mark the commencement of a split between Millais' training and his interests, a parallelism in his artistic studies which later emerges as a major determinant of his mature work as well as, one could argue, a formative element in his eventual contribution to the Brotherhood.

Most of Bessell's tuition was concerned with the copying of engravings.[2] For this reason, perhaps, the child was quick to grasp, even at this early stage, some formal techniques. He executed one or two sharply observed portraits in which the tonal effect is calculated and impressive, background shading is used to offset the contour of the profile and details of the coat-collar are only lightly stated so as not to detract from the likeness. In copying a Classical head (fig.3.1) he was able to use two different pencil techniques: soft shading for the face and neck and a more defined and partly linear technique for the forms of hair ringlets. His observational skills were excellent; a number of diminutive but well-detailed studies have survived

of soldiers, carts and horses, the latter in foreshortened perspective (fig.3.2). These are drawn lightly in sepia wash with subtle eloquence beyond their immediate informational content. He was capable too of switching from liquid to linear media without real difficulty, even though the illustrations he undertook for *Fidelio* tell one more about the cultural conventions and constraints upon art of the time than they do about his sensitivity, perception and uniqueness. Perhaps Bessell's tuition was too prescriptive for the young Millais, in terms of his illustrative work. Certainly it was in the observational sketches, including portraits, that the child seems to have felt more comfortable (see fig.3.3).

It is known that Millais received much encouragement and adulation from those around him. He enjoyed displaying his drawing skills to family, friends and the soldiery whom he drew, and in later years to fellow-students: 'His precocious artistic gifts went together in a remarkable way with angelic good looks, which undoubtedly enhanced the impression he created, especially with adults.'[3] The ultimate act of encouragement on the part of the Millais family was to move the household to London so that he could study there, beginning as a nine-year-old at Sass's Academy. At that point he was already a prolific artist. It is not possible to distinguish, in the work of his eighth year, the continuing Jersey drawings from those made under tuition at the Academy. Some of the formal anatomical studies may have resulted directly from Bessell's teaching; they indicate the fine control of the pencil of which he was capable by this time; they lack the overworking of shadow, to the point of glazing the paper unpleasantly with graphite, of which he had been guilty in earlier work. This newly learned restraint is evident particularly in his copy, at eight years, of a work called *Two Children Embracing* (fig.3.4).

An account of the curriculum and teaching at the Sass school is given in the autobiography of artist W. P. Frith, who attended the school some years before Millais.[4] From his own experience he describes the considerable time spent on drawing, the sequence of assignments and the generally repressive regime. First, pupils learned to draw from other drawings from the Antique, a process known as 'drawing from the flat'. Then they studied the effect of light on a simple object such as a white plaster ball or some plaster grapes. 'Stumps' (pointed rolls of paper used to soften and smear the medium) were not allowed for this; the finer gradations of tone had to be accomplished unaided. When these tasks had been successfully accomplished, pupils graduated to working directly from the Antique, initially from small features and only later from the whole figures.

3.2 John Everett Millais, *Soldiers at Dinant*, 1836 (age 7)

3.3 John Everett Millais, *Portrait of John Evamy*, 1837 (age 8)

3.4 John Everett Millais, *Two children embracing*, 1837 (age 8)

This rigorous stepped approach to learning to draw and to a disciplined and highly conventional manner of drawing was further complemented by more specific studies; outline drawings from the works of accepted Masters such as Michelangelo, Poussin and the artist-teacher Carracci were laboriously produced. Any attempts at imaginative drawing were deplored and discouraged; if linked with the work of unfavoured artists they might even (and as happened in at least one case) result in expulsion.

In terms of what it set out to do, the tuition was impressively successful, as can be evidenced from the the young Millais' achievements at the school. One of his drawings, a study from an Antique bust of a warrior (fig.3.5) reveals the most astonishing tenacity of purpose in a child of nine years. It is executed in chalk and so finely delineated through tonal shading and highlighting as to convey not only the three-dimensionality but all the surface quality of the original bust. For this drawing, Millais won the Gold Medal of the Society of Arts. Another drawing in the same year, *Bannockburn* (fig.3.6), shows in its stylized forms of prancing horses the consequences of his studies in the National Gallery; it won him the Society's Silver Medal.

Drawings which Millais made at ten years while still a pupil at Sass's Academy reinforce the notion of two complementary halves of his activity, a phenomenon which persisted into his adolescence. Two sheets of drawings of armoured soldiers, one with pikes and swords in a battle scene (fig.3.7) and another in a more peaceful interior reveal that his tutors were guiding him towards the heroic figure compositions regarded as the most prestigious subject-matter for contem-

3.5 John Everett Millais, Bust of a warrior (from the Antique), 1838 (age 9)

porary artists. But, in the former, a small and much more spontaneous drawing at the bottom of the page seems to ruminate on past pleasures of observing the soldiers on the beach at St Helier or Dinan; the second sheet similarly contains a light impromptu sketch of a small fortified tower.

Millais' parents showed their son's sketchbooks to the then President of the Royal Academy, Sir Martin Archer-Shee. Although sceptical about the potential of such a young pupil, he was impressed by the quality of achievement and accepted him into the Academy Schools. Millais entered as its youngest ever student at eleven years. Frith was already there himself when the prodigy arrived:

I can well remember the amusement of the students – some of whom were then, as now, almost middle-aged men – when a little handsome boy, dressed in a long blue coat confined at the waist by a black leather band, walked into the Antique School and gravely took his place amongst us.[5]

In a speech made when he was an Academician, Millais romanticized his early memories of the Academy Schools: 'I love everything belonging to it – the casts I have drawn from as a boy, the books I have consulted in the Library, the very benches I have

3.6 John Everett Millais, *Bannockburn*, 1836 (age 9)

3.7 John Everett Millais, Battle scene and sketch, 1839 (age 10)

3.8 John Everett Millais, *News of the defeat of the Royalists*, 1840 (age 11)

sat on – I love them all.'[6] But it was at that time and for many years an inflexibly organized institution, not easily amenable to change and with rigidly controlled Schools of study in the Antique, Life Drawing (described as 'from nature'), Painting, Perspective and Architectural Drawing. Any student wishing to undertake drawing from life had first to study for at least three years in the Antique School.[7] Millais had to wait much longer because of his extreme youth. He subsequently claimed that the teaching in the Antique School was inadequate; teachers pointed out defects of proportion in students' drawings but 'without at the same time calling attention to the principles of proportion and demonstrating the actions of the muscles'. He wanted the living model to be constantly present 'so that agreement or difference between nature and the Antique might be studied'.[8]

He also claimed that having 'entered when very young … finding that there was no teaching, I very soon ceased to attend'. He attended just long enough (he said) 'to satisfy myself that I could learn quite as easily without attending the Academy'.[9] This probably

means, and his work suggests, that he avoided the actual classes and teachers but still attended in the sense of using the facilities, choosing some activities rather than others (where permissible) and absorbing his observations of the work of his fellow-students. He worked a great deal from the Antique but also made studies of skeletal anatomy and some compositions. An example of the latter is *News of the defeat of the Royalists* (fig.3.8), a drawing in pencil and sepia wash which shows that he was not immune at this time from the problems of relating perspective to composition; figures, furniture and walls are awkwardly juxtaposed. An odd feature of this work which is not accounted for by these problems is also the presence of a diminutive but otherwise fully adult figure reclining in the foreground and giving the drawing a medieval quality without apparent meaning.

Millais may have avoided most of the teaching because of its poor quality but it seems unlikely that he would have failed to respond to the advice of good artist-teachers in the Academy. However, four years before he had entered it, the artist J. M. W. Turner had

3.9 John Everett Millais, Drawing of part of the Parthenon frieze, 1843 (age 14)

3.10 John Everett Millais, *Chinese from Macao*, 1842 (age 13)

resigned from his post as 'Professor of Perspective' there, because 'his lectures were often neglected'.[10] But while Millais was a student, Turner was a frequent 'Visitor' (visiting teacher). Although primarily a landscape painter, his appointments were always to the Life School. Students (such as Edwin Landseer) greatly respected the teaching in this field that they received from him.[11] But evidently Turner's skills in landscape painting were not directly available to students. The skills of others may have been inaccessible for different reasons; many were as irresponsible in discharging their duties as students were in attending lectures.

Although the Academy was unhelpful to the young Millais in the medium of oils, he began at this time to experiment with them. In general he executed work on a widening range of subject-matter as well as in a broad range of media. There was no encouragement from tutors for this; their tuition was inflexible. But Warner argues that Millais was eager to acquire Royal Society medals, which could not normally be awarded more than once to any artist for work in the same medium or subject-matter.[12] He 'proceeded to carry off every prize for which he entered', according to Geoffroy Millais,[13] an achievement which, as Frith pointed out, guarantees nothing in itself about eventual worth as an artist. Frith described a fellow-student at the Academy, who had won numerous medals but who subsequently failed as an artist.[14]

Millais, however, had qualities which went beyond the mere ability to produce appropriate work to win medals, but the fact of the nature of the awards does show how a student's training at the Academy and the judgements of tutors did not necessarily encourage or measure the most importantly useful attributes and achievements.

The collection of Millais' early drawings reveals a probably covert widening of his activities at this time. After two years of study in the Academy's constrained environment, a growing number of sketches from nature show a reaffirmation of his interest, which originated in early childhood, in the observation and recording of natural forms. There are soft pencil sketches, made at thirteen years, of rocks and sheep, and a powerful watercolour at the same time, *Study of a rock* (pl.III). Judging by the subject-matter and medium they were probably made away from the Academy. Meanwhile for Academy tutors he was producing conventional compositions of themes from Classical mythology or from history. The Academy may not have actively discouraged work from nature but it did not encourage it and probably no one there saw the rural sketches.

This division of interests and its eventual outcome make the sequential study of the early Millais drawings of great significance to education as well as to art. Reacting against the attitudes within the Academy while also embracing the artistic conventions of the period, Millais must have felt a sense of freedom and excitement when there was time on his own to explore nature; it may account, as Warner believes,[15] for the presence of so much detail from nature in many of his major works as a mature Pre-Raphaelite artist. Certainly as an adolescent student and artist he worked in two increasingly distinct worlds.

3.11 John Everett Millais, *Hebe (a racehorse)*, 1844 (age 15)

3.12 John Everett Millais, *Gildston*, 1844 (age 15)

In the world of studentship he became obediently more adept at drawing from the Antique, using the conventional pastel, chiaroscuro and monochrome techniques. His compositions seem graceful, flowing and linear in pencil or alternatively more stilted and formal if executed in wash. Adopting styles from others appears to have been a useful strategy for development; he produced a series of studies of Classical figures drawn with thick left-side lines and thin right-side lines which evoke the qualities of the Neo-Classicist sculptor John Flaxman's (1755–1826) bas-relief work. (Flaxman had himself been a student at the Academy some 70 years earlier.) It seems strange that an artist as assured as Millais felt the need to imitate in this way, but copying was in any case a respected activity of the time and the Academy perhaps an inhibiting place to study, even for a student of such initial strength as the young Millais (fig.3.9).

In the world of private study, the skills so rigidly exploited by the Academy's curriculum became the free servants of Millais' delighted observation; here he used pencil or pen and ink in a less linear way to create texture and to mould surfaces. Unfettered by the concept of monochrome, he found the flexibility and flow of watercolour capable of subtle colour nuances which might more fully express his observations. He found he could actually draw with colour (fig.3.10).

There was perhaps, by the age of thirteen, a real tension for Millais between the two worlds. In a drawing of a scene at Southampton Races, probably remembered, he used watercolour in a flat and literal manner very unlike his multi-tinted study of a rock in

the same medium and probably done the same year (pl.iii). It is as though he could not bring himself at that time to apply his more expressive and exciting technique to this conventional composition of horses and riders.[16]

Millais came increasingly to use watercolour at fourteen and fifteen years; he found it suitable for indicating the silkiness of a horse's hide (fig.3.11) as well as to use more decoratively in, for instance, his illustration of *Gildston* (fig.3.12). But during his studentship at the Royal Academy, it may never have been a medium that was much, if at all, encouraged even though one of the Academy's most eminent professors, Turner, was its foremost exponent. Since its inception, the Academy had denied the full significance of the watercolour medium,[17] so much so that watercolour painters were obliged to found their own institution.

Millais' prowess with the pencil grew steadily. The flowing sensual quality of earlier compositions became strongly stylized in the work which he executed while imitating Flaxman, such as the illustration done at thirteen years, *Godwin serving as a guide to Ulf* (and the same style seems to have encroached on his later study at age fourteen of the Parthenon frieze. But by sixteen he had almost managed to shake off this adopted style and to confidently reassert his own much more deft one in a sketch for *Non Angeli* (fig.3.13). Here for the first time can be seen the fusion of the formal Academy style with some of his own private and hitherto separate drawing experience, in the freshness of line and the swift sketching-in of smaller details. At this

3.13 John Everett Millais, Sketch for *Non Angeli*, 1845 (age 16)

3.14 John Everett Millais, *Palm trees*, 1845 (age 16)

3.15 John Everett Millais, *Brigands surprised,* 1846 (age 17)

3.16 John Everett Millais, *Male nude with sword*, 1846
(age 17)

time too he produced an eloquent study of palm trees
(fig.3.14), which by the nature of its poetic line seems
more akin to the twentieth than the nineteenth century;
it shows how confident he was becoming in his own
skills.

Millais was seventeen years of age and a capable
illustrator (fig.3.15) before the Academy permitted
him to draw from the life model. By then he was more
than ready to engage in this ultimate challenge for the
artist. One life-drawing at seventeen shows just a little
of his initial hesitation, a feeling that it exudes from all
the years of drawing from the lifeless Antique which
preceded it, by its static nature, uncanny smoothness
and uncompromising contour lines. Another is a
powerful though sensitive image: the model seems to
surge forward, muscles apparently tensed and the contour lines working with the form rather than merely
encompassing it two-dimensionally (fig.3.16). Nothing
that Millais accomplished in drawing at any time later
in his life exceeds this study in observational or
aesthetic skill.

In spite of this exceptional achievement (for his
years) in drawing the human figure, it is possible to
argue that the greatest successes of Millais' life's work
are not in his figure compositions and portraits, or
perhaps only in those where the figure is in some way
subservient to a background redolent with nature. In
the case of *Ophelia*, painted when Millais was in his
early twenties, the paradox of a living effigy of Ophelia
floats but also clearly drowns in a watery death-bed,
exotic with exquisitely drawn natural forms; a tapestry
of tiny plants and flowers turns a theme of death into
an almost celebratory lament for life.

In *Chill October*, painted when the artist was entering
his forties, the detail is not so precise and there are no
figures. This landscape is an aesthetic and mystical
evocation not only of natural forms but of natural conditions, of water reflecting the sky, of wind implied by
the curve of foliage and the movement of birds. It is a
richly dark painting, too, which makes full use of the
blending of viridians and umbers to create somnolent
shadow. The details of natural form are important but
subservient to the greater demands of the painting as a
single coherent and poetic statement. It is a work as far
removed as one might imagine from the teaching of
the Royal Academy. The Schools had helped him to
extend his already prodigious skills of draughtsmanship and composition. They fortunately never succeeded in extinguishing his brilliant expressive passion
for the first-hand study of nature, which became so
important in his mature 'Pre-Raphaelite' paintings,
even when subordinated to their central themes.

4

Privilege, opportunity and misfortune in the making of an artist: Henri de Toulouse-Lautrec (1864–1901)

Lautrec from birth had the gift; he drew and used pencil, a colour, like drink, like food – it was a need within him.

Maurice Joyant (1926)

The catalogue of the life's work of Henri de Toulouse-Lautrec by M.-G. Dortu lists over 3000 known preserved drawings for the artist's early work up to the age of eighteen years.[1] This is a remarkable output, something like two drawings for every three days from the age of six when records begin, and then even if the listings are comprehensive. In spite of this prolific record, the young Lautrec rarely referred to this active interest in his many letters, although once when about eight, writing from the Château du Bosc, he asked his mother to 'Please bring me four drawing board pins for spares'.[2] He did, however, illustrate many letters, a practice common to many talented and imaginative young people.

The Dortu catalogue may not be entirely comprehensive. Lautrec's drawings and paintings are more widely distributed than most, throughout Europe and North America, in public and private collections; private owners often conceal details of what they own. Even for such esteemed artists, childhood work, retained initially only from curiosity or family sentiment, may attract minimal interest. The catalogue affords an exceptionally generous inventory of Lautrec's earliest formative work, yet the drawings of that period have not so far attracted the kind of interest shown to Picasso's early work by its detailed chronological presentation in Barcelona.

Lautrec's childhood letters and drawings suggest their author as an affectionate and sensitive member of a large and scattered family, anxious to obtain responses to that affection and frequently separated from those he most loved. His family were wealthy French aristocrats, owners of vast vineyards and pine forests as well as several different châteaux. His holidays were spent in their various locations; he convalesced from illnesses in some and was sent away from one or another at times to be tutored. Children growing up in large households, especially without siblings, often report having felt marginalized and lonely. The young Henri, an only child, had numerous cousins and uncles, but not always where he happened to be. He was often separated and home-sick, particularly for his mother. But she it was who preserved many of his earliest drawings, indicating her interest as well as her diligence, not merely in saving sketchbooks and drawings from their places of origin in the various family homes, but also in conserving her son's many illustrated letters.

So far as is claimed, the preserved drawings represent the child Henri's drawing activity only from the age of six. Perhaps anything which he produced earlier seemed of insufficient skill to alert interest in the adults around him. Alternatively some may be inaccurately dated. Many young children display a confusing mix of precision, casualness, panache and gaucherie from day to day, which makes sequencing difficult. Lautrec's earliest works are no exception. Two sketches of boats are attributed to his seventh year, but arguably one of them could well be an earlier production. The drawings in a letter attributed to the same year by Goldschmidt and Schimmel[3] seem naive compared with the obviously more controlled and conceptually knowing *Têtes d'homme, de chevaux et chiens* (D20) and could also have been made at least a year earlier.

However, all the drawings alleged to have been created when Henri was six make a stunning group as evidence of the child's family and provincial surroundings. Claude Marks noted that 'as a child, Henri drew animals before he drew people',[4] but the drawings give a different view of an exceptionally diverse range of observations and imaginings. While horses, donkeys, hares and rabbits, flying birds and parrots, bears, fish, goats and monkeys appear in his first known work

4.1 Henri de Toulouse-Lautrec, *Animals and anthropomorphic figures* (D8), 1871 (age 6)

at (or before) six years, there are also cavalrymen, helmeted soldiers, devils, coachmen, huntsmen, children, cooks, bonneted ladies, servants and a great variety of other figures, busts and heads as well as at least one landscape with houses.

Some of the animals are attired anthropomorphically in uniforms and standing erect (see fig.4.1); some humans are caricatured. Other subjects include coaches, carts and harnesses, an umbrella, a kite and telescope, a trumpet, serving-dishes and their stands, as well as the boats mentioned earlier. While animals were clearly important and horses already paramount, they appear simultaneously within this much wider range of subject-matter.

Although the six-year-old Lautrec was living in some isolation from wider cultural and particularly urban influences, he could have been affected by popular imagery from publications available at the time and to which he may have had access, such as the then widely circulated *Images d'Epinal* from the publishers 'Imagerie Pellerin' (fig.4.2). It has been suggested that many of Lautrec's contemporaries in France, including Courbet, Manet, Gauguin and Seurat, were so influenced.[5] Of Seurat for instance, John Russell wrote that after the artist's death 'sixty-one pieces of imagerie populaire, primitive broad-sheets dating largely from the 1840's were found in his studio; these must have shown him, already in childhood, how to simplify an image and give it an abrupt monumental quality'.[6]

Lautrec's drawings at age six do indeed seem to show such an influence. The anthropomorphic charac-

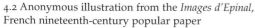

4.2 Anonymous illustration from the *Images d'Epinal*, French nineteenth-century popular paper

4.3 Henri de Toulouse-Lautrec, *Bonne fête* (D21), 1871 (age 6)

ters in some drawings are akin to subject-matter in the printed papers and the poses of certain figures are similar too. In drawings such as *Bonne fête* (fig.4.3) (though this may be somewhat later), he also echoed styles from the illustrated papers, tapering human legs for a slightly comic effect. This recurs in later drawings, such as a caricature of a man done at eleven (D462), and in a sketch as a fifteen-year-old of duellists, where it serves to convey their lightness of foot (D1768). These strategies, so early assimilated, became habitual and eventually characteristics of much of his mature work; in *Chocolat dancing*, of 1895 (fig.4.4), legs are similarly tapered, the feet angled, pointed and expressively positioned.

Nevertheless, it would be wrong to link too much of the child's image-making with secondhand sources.

He was growing up in a world where there was much to observe and to excite him, especially in terms of animals. And there was a strong family tradition of drawing and painting, with horses as the prime theme. While he imbued rabbits with human behaviour and dressed dogs in military uniforms, as the comic papers prompted him to do, he was making drawings from observation which for all his dexteral inexperience were far more expressively sophisticated.

What clearly fascinated him at this time was the impression of movement, such as he would have gained from frequent observations of hunting parties in the woods and fields around one of the family homes, in which members of his family participated. Fleeting glimpses of groups of riders galloping fast across the landscape were recreated by his pencil as

4.4 Henri de Toulouse-Lautrec, *Chocolat dancing*, 1895
(oils, blue crayon and Conté crayon, 65 × 50 cm; now
in the Musée Toulouse-Lautrec, Albi)

4.5 Henri de Toulouse-Lautrec, *Cavaliers and animals* (D7), 1871 (age 6)

organized compositions in which the startled animal- and bird-life he witnessed also play their part (see, for example, fig.4.5). These tentative and racily conceived images are full of raw energy and owe nothing to example. It is their immediacy which courts the eye from within a casual drawerful of mixed sketches by him, his cousins and uncles at the Château du Bosc. Theirs are conventionally interesting; his are of the soul.

When he was not focusing on animal mobility, Henri's observations of people around him were understandably more controlled and formal; he could select a style to fit circumstance, such as in the delicate drawings, possibly done from memory, of horses and a horse-drawn cart (D2) and other horses' heads (D20). Portraying character, an early preoccupation, was to become a life's theme; in D21 (fig.4.3) he was already analysing what makes one human being appear so

different from another: the shape of legs, clothing of different design, corpulence or slenderness. In a more interactive study (D13), human figures with long noses appear to be playing jokes on each other.

This, then, is the early base of Henri's drawing experience before his seventh birthday and the seeding of later developments: a combination of eclecticism, absorbed perhaps unconsciously, with an unusually uninhibited and instinctive thrust towards an impressionist rather than literal view. This is particularly interesting, given the object-centred and traditional approach of those of his family who were his artistic, albeit amateur, exemplars. The child exhibited a fluency not only of execution but of perception, which made him intensely responsive to the aesthetic of a drawing and to its media and often also to the whole event of an experience rather than to its constituent parts.

4.6 Henri de Toulouse-Lautrec, *Jument et Poulain* (D29), 1873 (age 8)

4.7 Henri de Toulouse-Lautrec, *The trainer* (D100), c.1874 (age 10)

In 1872, when Henri was seven years of age, he moved for a while to live in Paris, initially with his parents. Although this was the year of the first Paris Impressionist exhibition, there is no evidence in his drawings or letters that he or his family were at the time aware of that momentous event in the history of art or that it had any effect upon their attitudes to art. No doubt a prime purpose of the move was to acquire a suitable education for the child, found initially at the Lycée Fontanes.

Paris was a heady experience for him; he wrote of having 'a good time' there although he missed the familiarity of Bosc. He settled cheerfully enough into his school and liked his tutor, Mr Mantoy, describing in his letters his good friendships with other boys, attending a puppet-theatre performance and enjoying the company of an older female cousin also in Paris.[7] But he was still glad to return to Bosc and Céleyran on vacation.

Surviving drawings from these days are imprecisely dated; Dortu lists several sketchbooks as covering a lengthy period between the ages of eight and seventeen. Only three drawings here are specified for the age of eight, another fifteen for between eight and ten, and two for the age of nine. Precise dating is further complicated by the problem of distinguishing between observed and remembered subject-matter; the probability is that a child so fluent in drawing from imagination as well as from observation would frequently work from memory. The known interests of the young Lautrec at the time are the best clues to inferring the chronology of the sketchbooks.

The three specifically eight-year-old drawings are very different in apparent facility. D27 is a stilted picture of a horse and rider and D28 is a silhouette of a wolf, poorly formed. They are both so little like the vigorous sketch of two wild horses, *Jument et Poulain* (fig.4.6), that their authenticity as well as their chronology could well be doubted, were it not for the realization that extreme variations of style and performance characterize the whole of Henri's development as an artist. Indeed, in D30 (of the eight-to-ten-year group), the characteristics of D28 (heavily shaded ground), D27 (position of the horse's legs) and D29 (delicate but lively contours) blend as if to confirm authorship of all three other drawings.

Tentative links with events are possible. Two months after his eighth birthday, Henri wrote from Paris to one of his favourite cousins, Madeleine Tapié de Céleyran, describing his excitement at visiting an American circus, 'where I saw eight elephants who walked on their heads. There was a cageful of lions....'[8] At this time too, Mr Mantoy was encouraging him to draw from first hand in the Paris zoo. A sketchbook of drawings loosely designated 1874–80 (D95 to D173) contains a number of pencil sketches apparently made from direct observation of zoo animals. There are also two graphic though tentative impressions of an animal trainer (fig.4.7) with his lions, perhaps done from memory.

Similar subject-matter does indeed recur frequently in other vaguely dated sketchbooks, but in some of those (for example an album dated 1875–78, D174–D178) the work is often in pen and seems less spontaneous, more calculating, as though the outcome of repetition and refinement rather than recent memory. This suggests that the former album may be more nearly defined as being from 1874–75 when the young artist was nine or ten years of age (a belief adhered to

4.8 Henri de Toulouse-Lautrec, *Homme d'affaires* (D371),
1876 (age 11)

by the late owner of the album and descendant of the
Lautrec family, Mme de Villefort), with the latter perhaps accounting for the two or three following years.

There are also sketchbooks which reveal very mixed
ideas and treatment, so that accurate and reliable
dating is indeed difficult. The entire group of ninth-
to-eleventh-year drawings contains such variety: there
are some casual drawings of rabbits, one with a rabbit
ensconced in a cooking pot and with a half-human
figure beside it (D42) which reflects the content of an
Images d'Epinal paper. There are also skilful pages of
figure studies which compare personalities and some
sharp caricatures of angular or obese men. A study of
a seated figure awkwardly captures the pose but omits
some features as though encountering difficulty (D36).
One much more articulate study of a woman elegantly
posed and dressed suggests that, like many young
artists, Henri may have been copying Classical paintings (D44) or was at least influenced by them; the
figure is reminiscent of Terborch.

Since drawings D353 to D376 are identified specifically as being from Henri's eleventh year (1876), they
provide us (if that is the case) with some positive indications of his skills and interests for that period, when

he had already been in Paris for three years. He had
studied at the Lycée Fontanes (now Condorcet) and at
another school. Ill-health caused periodic returns to
Albi. The year before he had needed treatment for his
leg muscles and separate tutoring was necessitated.
He was already influenced by the equestrian paintings
of Princeteau, who had taught his father, and he was
much impressed by Princeteau's new painting of a
racehorse.[9]

The drawings of this time include some illustrated
letters, further sketches of horses and riders, observations of animals, including melodiously flowing
drawings of horses, such as D373, and various giraffes,
bison, pelicans and seals, no doubt generated by his
current zoo studies. A better-known drawing, *La
Bécasse* (D360) shows an awareness, perhaps, in its
concept and detail of the Dutch still-life tradition; that
is why it is better known. As with earlier examples,
some of Henri's twelfth-year figure drawings from
memory (such as D372) seem more awkward and less
coordinated than those of his animal subjects. One
curiously prophetic drawing shows a bearded heavy-
bodied and short-legged horseman (*Hommes d'affaires*,
fig.4.8).

The diversity of both style and standard continues in the drawings of the year of his thirteenth birthday (D638–D667). Some if not all of them might have been created before the first of the two crucial incidents in which he appeared to have damaged his legs, although a congenital bone condition was later recognized. Excellent pen sketches of sailing boats, probably from direct observation, demonstrate a fresh eye and familiarity with masts and sails. The customary racing, jumping or prancing horses are drawn now with a panache quite superior to their equivalents from the pen of Henri's father, le Comte Alphonse.[10]

There is humour again in some drawings of animal-masked people (D645 and D646); more serious drawings, for example of huntsmen, use some of the same caricatural devices previously noted, but with more subtlety to suggest character rather than absurdity. Such expressive techniques appear to anticipate those employed in the artist's maturity, such as in sketches entitled the *Quadrille of the Louis XIII chair at Elysée Montmartre*, which he drew when he was twenty-one years of age, or the crayon drawing *Chocolat dancing* (fig.4.4) which was executed ten years later.

Two sketches in a totally different idiom from anything else in this phase of Henri's development, and which are remote too from the conventions of the time, are strong jocular profiles, one of which could be argued to anticipate the artistic style of twentieth-century comic-books as yet undrawn (D659). Outstanding in this group are two illustrated pages in his schoolbooks, more eloquent and, in the case of D659, wittier than any other drawing in this year group; the other (D638) is a fine example of Henri's skill with a pen and also shows him at his most confident, drawing a table and figures with two different but complementary linear styles to differentiate knowingly between fixed and fleeting forms. It is in sharp contrast with a sketch of the same subject made three to five years earlier (D36).

By the age of fourteen, the artist appears to have been deeply aware of the sensuality of the media he was using, usually pencil or pen. The hundred or so drawings preserved from that period seem more consciously artistic, reflecting an enlarging appreciation of the full range of subject-matter of artists generally: still-life, the nude, figure composition, serious portraiture and historical scenes. And in his own portraits he had begun to combine a sense of form with a sense of texture (D829), moving well beyond his earlier predominantly linear work.

A large number of zoo animals were drawn in his fifteenth year, a fact which does not obviously fit with his known situation at this age. The first of his 'accidents' would by now have occurred and these drawings may have been completed between the two accidents or, in some cases, after the second one. He is known to have drawn extensively while bedridden and his ability to produce dynamic impressions from memory is undeniable.

After the second mishap, he spent time recuperating in Nice, making more rich pen sketches of sailing vessels such as the probably earlier *Three boats* (fig.4.9) and D833. At this time he wrote of seeing 'quite a few merchant vessels and an English yacht that is a veritable jewel'[11] although making no mention of seeing any zoo animals. It is likely and possible that while he was immobilized he would have reflected on times in Paris and was able to recreate observations made then. Some other drawings of the period, of figures in action (playing sedate games for example), exude a different flavour, as though drawn at first hand. Sharp caricatures (such as *Electrophage et Tanski* (fig.4.10)) are seldom absent for long from what was by this stage a considerable drawing record.

Mme de Villefort argued that Henri's enforced immobility was a decisive factor in orienting him towards drawing and painting, together with the counsel and example at this time of his uncle, Charles. To Charles he later wrote, 'It was you who lit in me the flame of drawing'.[12] But it was a flame that had already been kindled years before.

Dortu's catalogue raisonnée positions a large group of drawings vaguely between the ages of ten and fourteen years. But the subject-matter suggests that few of this group are from earlier than his fourteenth birthday and some possibly later. Legs are a recurring topic of interest. He may not at that time have realized the likely long-term consequences of his 'accidents'; he had fallen and broken a femur but the underlying causes were congenital. He must have been preoccupied with the incapacitation and apprehensive too. Trying to make light of the problem, he wrote from Albi in July 1878, describing a special donkey-carriage which had been made to give him some mobility as 'a chariot drawn by a fiery horse' and signing himself 'your crutch-walking godson'.[13]

Since the incapacitation was only to his legs and there was no manual impairment, his drawing continued obsessively. In some sketches he studied the articulation of human limbs; he surrounded his French and Latin notes with some of legs and shoes, female as in D291, male in D293 and bare-legged in a letter with some drawings of legs (fig.4.11). In one sketchbook, in drawings D392–D585, there are various legs, running or leaping, with action clearly important. A small sketch (D480) shows the artist himself, just getting out of bed and trying to pull a sock onto a rather short limb; other drawings show him in bed. They are a poignant reflec-

4.9 Henri de Toulouse-Lautrec, *Three boats* (D832), c.1877 (age 12)

4.10 Henri de Toulouse-Lautrec, *Electrophage et Tanski* (D795), c.1879 (age 14)

4.11 Henri de Toulouse-Lautrec, Letter with drawings of legs (D298), c.1879 (age 14)

4.15 Henri de Toulouse-Lautrec, *Circus scene* (D1753), 1880 (age 15)

tion on his predicament, no doubt seen at the time as temporary and transient, but which was to have far-reaching consequences.

At fifteen years the artistic 'leap' seems gigantic, much influenced by a broadening conception of the nature of art: more intellectual in approach, more uniform in quality and achievement, more confident even than before. Nearly 200 drawings specifically for this year are recorded (D1620–D1819). Henri spent time in Céleyran, Bosc and Nice, to which latter place his family took him to escape the northern winter and to help the slow healing of his legs.[14]

Although some sketches are directly derived from a locality, such as *Grape-gathering at Céleyran* (fig.4.12) or *Fisherman in Nice*, D1369, many are of the independent themes of his developing skill as an artist and exist more as personal imagery than as reportage. The horses which at earlier stages were poems of animal movement now accentuate form and structure more than movement itself (D1693); this interest is emphatic in a study of a bull (D1748), although the racy, dramatic and effervescent animal sketches still appear at times. The same is true of drawings of human characters which continue on the one hand as comical (*Chez le coiffeur*, D1766) or action sketches (*Duel*, D1768) not greatly changed from similar much earlier drawings; on the other hand there are serious academic studies of individuals with all the interplay of line and mass, light and shade, texture and smoothness which might be expected of an experienced and conventional art student of the period (D1625 and D1626). By the following year, when he was sixteen, he was able to produce an accomplished study in oils, *Artilleryman saddling his horse*, for which an exceptionally solid drawing (fig.4.13) is probably a preparatory sketch.

A development of future significance at this point was an interest in the portrayal of female elegance. In a delicate sketch, *Elégante* (fig.4.14), a woman stands poised in a flowing gown and a strikingly large hat; her light long scarf floats behind her. The circus theme returns in *Circus scene* (fig.4.15), a firm dynamic contour-drawing of a tiger and trainer. There are first indications too of a style of drawing which was to come into its own in the *Cocotte* series a year later (see *Et galope, et galope*, fig.4.16); like D1779 this reveals a developing technique of pen cross-hatching to enrich form and surface. New also for the young Lautrec are some experiments with figureless compositions using pencil and white chalk on a middle-tone (blue-grey) paper (for example, D1784). Human appearance continued to intrigue him; there is a portrait only slightly exaggerated of a top-hatted 'dandy' (D1819), some caricatures of nude fat men (D1793) and another of a large-headed short-legged man playing the flute and surrounded by several classically drawn male legs (D1679).

At the age of fifteen to sixteen years, the volume of Lautrec's drawing activities was escalating, with a corresponding diversification of style, subject-matter and technique, commensurate with his serious commitment to study and in spite of intermittent physical difficulties. Nevertheless, at sixteen he tended to belittle his own activities as an artist. He spent some time at Céleyran during the winter, where he wrote of 'fooling around with St. Palette'.[15] In summer he went south to recuperate, this time at Lamalon-les-Bains where he claimed, 'there isn't anything interesting here', but went on to advocate that someone else, if they could draw, might 'fill a whole album with all the grimaces of the guests drinking the waters'.[16] Curiously he makes no mention at this time of the important drawings he was making for his friend Etienne Devismes' story, *Cocotte*.[17]

The drawings for *Cocotte* (a story about an old man) are all in pen, making much use of Lautrec's recently acquired technique of hatching and cross-hatching. Some figures are caricatured (the fat priest), others

4.16 Henri de Toulouse-Lautrec, *Cocotte: Et galope, et galope* (D2030), 1881 (age 16)

drawn naturally (the helmeted soldiers) or with great simplicity (children). A sense of deep space is created by making the foreground figures contrastingly large. Strong tonal contrasts often emphasize the central figures in these dynamic compositions and actual silhouetting also aids composition (D2035) or heightens atmosphere (D2041). The illustrations are planned for sequential effect, making use of 'close-up' devices when the story would benefit from it; D2031 looks like a close detail of part of the action from *Et galope, et galope*.

These drawings stand a little apart from most of Henri's work of the period, even though he was utilizing ideas and techniques familiar within it. His pen had certainly not superseded his use of the pencil, which continued to be constantly active. His drawings remained generally small in scale, with the drawing-paper seldom more than eight inches in its longest dimension. Like many artists at any age he could be inhibited on occasions; a portrait of his cousin Raoul is strangely dull and poorly modelled (D1911) yet another sketch, of a man seated by a fireplace, is deft and spirited, very much a precursor in style of good twentieth-century caricature (D1941).

At sixteen, and with a small number of competent

paintings in oils behind him, Lautrec's sketchbook drawings had begun to assume a different role in his artistic activity, many drawings being deliberately initiated with paintings in mind. A drawing in charcoal on canvas of a knight, D2000, extends the theme of innumerable early sketches into an atmospheric and classical formal composition, perhaps with the intention of taking it further in oils. At this time too, compositions and not merely individual figures were much redrawn and restated to refine the idea and the image (see for example D2005, D2009, D2010). One such series shows an (as yet rare) interest in the symbolic; an anchor and a skull lie half concealed in the sand by the water's edge. Perhaps this was observed in Nice, perhaps imagined (D2006, *Oceana nox*).

In spite of his own disclaimers of interest, he was continually fascinated by the appearance of people around him. Some splendid caricatures of the visitors, like himself, to Nice accompany his observational sketches in a notebook, the *Cahier de Zig-Zag* (D2064–D2075). A study, wittily elongated, of two artificially posed English ladies (D2072) seems to anticipate the attenuations of a Giacometti sculpture.

When not resting or recuperating in Nice or at another of the family's holiday locations, Lautrec worked enthusiastically under the benevolent guidance of Princeteau, as a caricature of them both feverishly painting at their easels shows (fig.4.17). Dortu confidently places this drawing at sixteen years (1881), but other sources seem to date Lautrec's studentship with Princeteau from the following year.[18] However, he certainly studied formally in Paris prior to his seventeenth birthday, with the familiar pattern of observational, memory and imagined sketches continuing in the background, and the same diversity of styles. At this time he completed a series of very loose, almost tentative, but lively, drawings, full of caricature and action (see *Submersion*, D2160 to D2208), as well as some more detailed work.

A list of Henri's general subject-matter in his drawings at sixteen does not reveal so very many differences from the similar list of his work ten years previously, when he was six. He drew at sixteen dogs, ducks, captive birds, badgers, polecats, cattle, horses (usually in rapid movement), serious formal portraits, character sketches of heads, comic profiles, horsemen, soldiers, servants, peasants and sailors, carriages, sailing boats, landscapes (but only a few) showing bridges, for example, and a château (D2343, probably the Château du Bosc).

His portrayals of female figures continued to be fairly limited in number, although he was beginning to persevere with female portraits; D1925 is a study of a seated woman and two other drawings (D2378 and D2379) show quite severe caricatures of women. Much of the work consists of figures or objects without visual contexts and, as Joyant records, Henri, on his own admission in a letter to a friend in 1879, had come to avoid landscapes: 'I'm totally incapable of doing them, even the shadows; my trees are spinach and my sea looks like what you will.'[19]

Dortu places a group of 193 drawings (D2427 to D2619) in the period 1881–83 (sixteen to eighteen years) when Lautrec was becoming physically stronger and in consequence even more active as an art student. In this group there are numerous accomplished formal life studies, executed mainly in charcoal or pencil and with strong flat areas of light and shade seeming rather to anticipate the flat planes of Cubism which were not themselves to be defined as such for a further 25 years. Allowing for periods of vacation, these life drawings could have been completed at the rate of three per week over the two-year period and clearly represent great energy and effort as well as development in technique. Drawing from the Antique was far less frequent (D2612, D2618, D2608).

Lautrec's portrait at seventeen years of Madame Béatrix Tapié de Céleyran (D2631), a charcoal drawing with an angular pattern of light and shade, strongly

three-dimensional, shows the value of the intensive life studies. Subsequent drawings are both larger and more powerful. They include carefully posed and executed portraits of Lautrec or the de Céleyran family members. This was a year when portraits and full-figure studies were obviously of consuming interest. In the family portraits and in other portraits of anonymous servants and labourers, the search was clearly for the essence of character but by now with all the authority and knowledge gained from hours spent in the life room. Expression was of paramount importance in D2724, the quality of line more so in D2727, and in the detail of the beard in D2735; fig.4.18 is a fine, searching and revealing self-portrait. Lautrec was by now working in Bonnat's studio, but moved on to another tutor, Cormon, just before he was eighteen.

There are 95 drawings in the Dortu catalogue which, according to Dortu, are from the year following Lautrec's eighteenth birthday. Considered together, D2742 and D2750 highlight the two complementary approaches of this period of his work, the painterly and the illustrative, having the same subject-matter. The former drawing, of a man seated, employs the 'pre-Cubist' style of the life drawings (already mentioned) to create an image having its own aesthetic and artistic meaning beyond its subject content. The latter drawing, of a similar subject, strives to define the character through detailed observation of features and clothing, with medium and technique entirely subservient to this objective.

All the ingredients of Lautrec's earlier work are present in this group of drawings from his eighteenth year. There are various life and costume-life drawings of studio models, another (but bearded) self-portrait (D2817), a drawing of a vine-grower which achieves character by compressing the figure (D2832) and further caricatures of Princeteau. Some caricatures appear to compare the geometry of forms (D2824). Both meticulous and rapid drawing recur; a fine study of the Comte Alphonse (D2830) captures his bulk and attitude, and the hands, heads and legs are racily investigated (D2776).

Richard Thomson writes that 'In the years between 1885 and 1891, Lautrec's painterly style was established; the distance between the relatively academic *Emile Bernard* of 1885 and the fully personal *Paul Sescau* of 1891, to take as examples two portraits, measures the artist's development.'[20] Yet what happened between those two years was perhaps no more than the confirmation of a style which had been developed over a much longer period through prolific activity, experiment and the absorption of many influences.

The fluent, expressive if undisciplined adventures of Henri's childhood pencil eventually combined with

4.17 Henri de Toulouse-Lautrec, *Princeteau and Lautrec* (D2077), 1881 (age 16)

4.18 Henri de Toulouse-Lautrec, *Self-portrait* (D2680), 1882 (age 17)

the formal skills he learned from his teachers (Mantoy, Princeteau and Bonnat) in Paris during his adolescence. The seeds of the mature style were already beginning to be sown when the six-year-old Henri scribbled his fleeting impressions of horses galloping across the family estates and when, as an invalid at thirteen, he was given more time than even he may have wanted to do nothing else but draw.

The enthusiasms of his childhood, such as the circus, remained lifelong interests, expressed for instance in *The bareback rider*, a crayon-and-wash drawing executed in 1899, just two years before his death. All the experimental and the more academic drawing can be seen united in the painting *A dance at the Moulin Rouge* of 1890. His preoccupation with caricature emerges constantly throughout his career as an artist, as in his unflattering study of Yvette Guilbert of 1894. And his intense adolescent pursuit of character through portraiture came to a brilliant peak in what Thomson aptly describes as the 'luminous portrait' of *Miss Dolly, The English girl from the Star, Le Havre*, painted in oils in 1899.[21]

It remains surprising that such an alert young artist was so little affected in adolescence by the contemporary Impressionist movement which was emerging around him. It was not until he was in his early twenties that he moved noticeably beyond the artistic conventions of home and studio and into a more contentious world of avant-garde art. But by this time he had as much as sixteen years of consistent experience in drawing, technique and expression, and the consequent artistic authority, to bring to his consideration of contemporary developments.

5

Early ambition and a vision of artistic nobility:
Pablo Ruiz Picasso (1881–1973)

'Ecole de dessin' should be emblazoned on every artist's door. Not however, 'Ecole de peinture'.

Picasso, c.1960

An essentially twentieth-century and still comparatively unusual phenomenon is represented in the attention paid by artists, historians and critics to the juvenile works of Picasso. At the beginning of the twenty-first century, he has remained the most widely known as well as the most controversial artist of his time, and the only one of such stature whose juvenile works have been seriously analysed for their significance as precursors of later achievements. Any mark made by Picasso at any time receives attention and has value, but few recognize the earliest drawings as significant works in their own right.

Picasso's own positive attitude to the relationship between the work of his childhood and that of his maturity, as well as the influence upon him and others of the child-art movement in Europe in the 1920s and 30s, make him a subject of particular importance in any consideration of early artistic development. This present investigation does not seek to replicate the many which precede it. Instead it focuses on the drawings and paintings created during the extraordinary period of artistic development between Picasso's ninth and sixteenth years, in order to assess the diverse claims of the relevant literature, and of the apocrypha. Secondly it speculates anew on the circumstances which may have predetermined the pace and nature of that period of the artist's development.

The plenitude of writings is both valuable and a problem. The phenomenon of Picasso is complex; the attitudes of his many biographers vary considerably. His friends idolize and mythologize, his women amplify or conceal, his critics theorize and those with a background in, for example, psychology, apply some of the stereotypes of that discipline to their explanation of a unique individual. The corporate outcome contains a variety of different judgements and interpretations.

Many only build their version of Picasso's early life and work upon the dramatic apocryphal stories, reinforced each time they are cited, that have come to illustrate his personality and account for his work. Picasso himself contributed to his own legend, imperfectly remembering and sometimes wilfully distorting the events and circumstances of his earliest years; it is suggested that his 'memories often involved an element of wish-fulfilment'.[1] Too many biographers have been deluded by his exaggerated recollections or those of his admirers. Only a few, Antonina Vallentin and John Richardson for instance, knew him well yet objectively enough to differentiate adequately between the likely and the improbable. Fortunately, the drawings, at least, speak their own truth.

Constantly reiterated are Picasso's claims that he had been an infant prodigy[2] and that as a child he could draw like Raphael.[3] Judging by the drawings from that time, neither of these claims seems quite justified. Picasso himself misrepresented the dates of some of the earliest drawings.[4] He is recorded as saying that he never *remembered* going through any drawing stage of 'awkwardness and naiveté' which might be associated with normal childhood and so he lamented the early academic precision which came at the expense of what he described as 'the genius of childhood'. But he also expressed a certain cynicism about those who taught the young, believing that, in the guise of freedom, children were constrained to draw as adults expected them to draw, rather than in whatever way they naturally evolved.[5]

Few of Picasso's childhood drawings done prior to eight years of age are in evidence. Although his father may have attributed minimal significance to those earliest naive works, Richardson infers that Picasso may later have destroyed many of them to suit his own arguments. Of the drawings which the artist eventually donated from his own childhood collection to the Museum in Barcelona, some do look as though they were made earlier. Most show vigour and a fresh eye, even if not the kind of spirited innocence which the mature Picasso would have liked to see. The drawings leave us guessing about any earlier allegedly prolific stages; he must have developed early on a facility to represent space and movement, but no more perhaps than many children in those years. The first available drawings, although they are lively images, are of mixed quality and might only have attracted attention at the time for their quantity.

Later in life, Picasso explained his reasons for having come to date most of his later artefacts, stressing the significance of time and place in the making of images: 'it's not sufficient to know an artist's works – it is necessary to know when he did them, why, how, under what circumstances',[6] and, he could perhaps have added, their sequence, the influence of the earlier upon the later. He envisaged his work as being like a diary, although it would be foolish of anyone to imagine that what the diary chronicles is only the truth; as John Richardson points out, diaries can have their fantasy elements or be in code.[7]

Gedo sees not just the images but also the emotions of early childhood as 'reverberant upon [Picasso's] art until the close of his career',[8] a view strongly supported by one of his racier biographers, Arianna Stassinopoulous-Huffington. The former, a psychologist, studies particularly the pressures and tensions of familial relationships in childhood; the latter, as a journalist, creatively interprets events and friendships.

Accounts of Picasso's childhood reveal him as a child rich in the problems that beset the prodigy as well as in prodigious skills. For many years he had to contend with a father who was both artist and teacher, who held rigid traditionalist views about painting and about teaching methods. As an only son, displaying early facility even if not great promise, he would have been especially vulnerable to his father's determination to teach him intensively and to plan his entire education as an artist.

It is recorded that the child drew and cut out pictures before he went to school (cut-out images remained a lifelong interest), having been encouraged to do so by his father to compensate for emotional difficulties in response to the birth of his first sister, Lola. The local school in Málaga accepted him when he was only just five. Art instruction there, according to Walther,[9] was derived from the linear-geometrical approaches of Pestalozzi and Froebel, which led on to the representation of forms through their abstraction from observation. Such a method would have tended to discourage the retention of what Walther calls 'a

truly childish way' of drawing but he suggests that 'it was that training that gave [Picasso] his astounding assurance in his craft' and argues for its valuable long-term consequences.[10] Certainly such first experiences are formative in most children; Pablo Ruiz (the name the family preferred to use at the time), however, was not to stay long at this particular school and, since he hated it, he is likely to have been unreceptive to its teaching and to that of the next one.

Surges of development as well as periods of near stasis are common in the lives of most individuals. The training initiated by Don José for his son, including the teaching in the Málaga school, appears to have generated an incredibly rapid period of development, startlingly represented in the sequence of works Picasso made between eight and fifteen years (bearing in mind that, with an October birthday, for most of the year 1890 the child was only eight years old).

The drawings at age eight look untutored. Picasso was interested in animals and in making quite small sketches of domestic ones: chickens, doves and dogs, in pencil or crayon, or sometimes as paper silhouettes; these are competent and, in the case of the doves, also show a feeling for movement and how to suggest it. In *Palomas* (fig.5.1, MPB 110.867),[11] a drawing executed in 1890, this is not so much apparent in the image of a flying dove with wings outstretched, but rather in other parts of the drawing where another bird is seen feeding its young; the larger and the group of small birds collectively give the impression of a bobbing action. Most of these sketches display practical and observational skill more than they reveal any special vision and expressive fluency.

While obviously learning fast, the boy appears to have been occasionally inhibited. Several writers draw attention to one of his first-known drawings of the human figure, a sketch made by Pablo Ruiz when he was only just nine, of *Hercules Wielding a Club* (fig.5.2). With clouded hindsight, Stassinopoulos-Huffington regards it as 'amazing for a child of this age',[12] but the figure is an unsophisticated, awkward and unremarkable version of the original, of which there was a statue in his home.[13] Much more significant – still gauche but freshly child-like – is his first-known oil painting *El Picador*: figures variously occluded behind the horse and the edge of the bull-ring effect a composition in depth. Though still an uneasy image, it is coherently interrelated.

While still only nine years old (during 1891), he was managing much better articulated figures, probably from memory and mostly scrawled around the edges of his schoolbook pages. In small sketches of a running bull, a caricature of a bull's head wearing a sombrero, a woman in a shawl with her arms akimbo, bulls about

5.1 Pablo Ruiz Picasso, *Palomas* (MBP 110.867), 1890 (age 8);
© Succession Picasso/DACS 2000

5.3 Pablo Ruiz Picasso, *Aldeanos y carro* (MBP 110.868), 1893
(age 11); © Succession Picasso/DACS 2000

5.2 Pablo Ruiz Picasso, *Hercules* (MBP 110.842), 1890 (age 9);
© Succession Picasso/DACS 2000

to fight, a priest and child, a scene with pigeons, a bull chasing a matador and a frontal view of a cat's head, he seems to set out his capabilities as an artist. The earlier awkwardness is largely superseded by rhythmic form; the figures convey mobility or strike attitudes.

Given the personal nature as well as the location of most of these sketches, illicitly inside schoolbooks, it is unlikely that his father had intervened in their making or even saw them at the time. The family had moved to La Coruña in April of that year and Pablo Ruiz became an informal pupil at the Instituto Da Guarda where his father now taught as well as at the local secondary school from which the schoolbooks came. While the father miserably accepted a climatically less benevolent town and a lesser post, the son flourished. By ten years of age he had considerably extended, repeated and improved his repertoire of drawing subjects, and the dogs, cats, pigeons, hares, bulls and people began to exhibit character differences; in the latter case, figures are differently dressed as musketeers or footsoldiers, and in some cases they are caricatured with detail. The occasional religious subject appears at this time. The quality of these images varies considerably, from the sharp, sophisticated observation shown in some of the caricatures to a crude sketch of the bust of a person; no doubt the artist found some subjects more engrossing than others.

In 1892, between his tenth and eleventh birthdays, now properly enrolled at the art school, the boy's formal education as an artist began in earnest, as the drawings show. His father's initiation of him into the formal techniques and traditions of drawing and painting was also beginning to take effect. Like a medieval apprentice, the child would be trusted to complete details of hands or pigeons for some of Don José's canvases, but the artist to whom he was 'apprenticed' was to prove barely adequate to the task.

Formal training did not stop more private drawing from continuing in the background, with the addition of some new subjects such as an Arab with a rifle, new situations (including some with religious themes: *Christ Crucified*, *The Passion of Christ*) and new techniques such as the silhouette, pre-empted by the cutout animal figures he had made a few years before. The cat reappears, this time with a neck, chest and front legs (*Croquis diversos*, MPB 110.930) and, although some think this to be a copied subject, it looks like a direct observation of an advancing animal. A detailed sketch, *Aldeanos y carro* (fig.5.3), also suggests such observation, of figures, animals and a wagon.

Compared with this illustration or some of the seated or standing male figures in the schoolbook margins, the portrayal of a person on the front of one of his Latin books for the same year appears crude.

Such sketches were probably considered experiments and expendable; other unrelated drawings are frequently superimposed in another plane on the same sheet; all that mattered, it seems, was to find a place to make them. In *La Corrida y seis estudios de palomas* (fig.5.4),[14] for example, the sketches of doves are upside-down in relation to the main picture.

But within this year, before he was eleven, some works are more formal, including a study of an acanthus flower and leaves (*Academia, flor de acanto*) and a copy of a drawing of an Antique torso (*Copiado de un vaciado en jeso*). These traditional subjects, conventionally executed, reveal his father's influence as well as that of the art school. The former drawing displays great linear control of essentially two-dimensional form and mastery of symmetry; the latter is more impressive, a 'tour de force' of charcoal and pencil, possibly a copy of another drawing, as was common in European art schools, but with all the gradations of tone necessary to convey a complex three-dimensional image in two dimensions. Whether working from the Antique or from copies of it, Pablo Ruiz clearly relished the task and would have enjoyed displaying his brilliance, even though he was working in charcoal and on a much larger scale than before. He quickly grasped techniques of fine shading and whatever his knowledge of anatomy was at the time, he managed almost to hew muscle and sinew out of the paper.

The spontaneously dynamic sketches like *Aldeanos y carro* now seem a better indicator of the nature of the boy's future achievement, but the panache of his performance in formal studies from the Antique would have been more significant to the disciplined artist that both Don José and the art school thought they were moulding. It was for those that he received accolades in his first examinations that year.

In 1893, at eleven years, he attempted two small oil paintings, both with an architectural farmhouse subject, *Casa de campo*. The first of these is a diffident study, where notions of perspective seem to have inhibited the task; it nevertheless shows an intelligent grasp of compositional issues, such as how to create a balance between foreground and background forms. The later attempt at the same subject shows a more sophisticated and natural composition, apparently arrived at with a greater understanding of the orchestration of tone, and with more intuition, less struggle and a proper artistic disregard for convention. He was learning fast from his own experiments.

A pen sketch, *Escena de una batalla* (fig.5.5), made at twelve to thirteen years, captures all the dramatic turmoil of the subject and demonstrates how much he could become involved with the human predicament,

5.4 Pablo Ruiz Picasso, *La corrida y seis estudios de palomas*
(MBP 110.869), 1892 (age 10); © Succession Picasso/DACS 2000

5.5 Pablo Ruiz Picasso, *Escena de una batalla* (MBP 110.610),
1893–94 (age 12–13); © Succession Picasso/DACS 2000

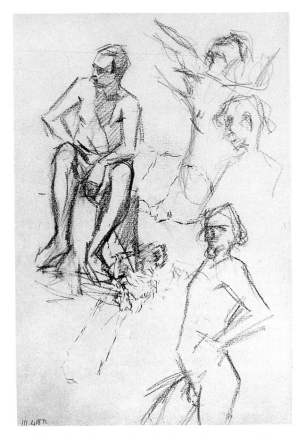

5.6 Pablo Ruiz Picasso, *Croquis diversos* (MBP 111.418R), 1894 (age 13); © Succession Picasso/DACS 2000

seems more important than the drawings themselves.[16]

The boy's twelfth birthday was in October 1893 and in the drawings which he created during the following year, 1894, both as student studies and independently, it is evident that this was a period when formal training and awareness of artistic conventions dominated over his more 'innocent 'eye'. He had the unusually early opportunity of being introduced to the study of the human figure, not only through the endless (and for him apparently effortless) examination of it from Antique sculpture, but also from the real thing; there are from this time a number of studies made directly from life, with poses simulating action (a figure pulling, swinging or throwing). Whereas the studies from the Antique of arms, feet or torsos are intensively and investigatively overworked, as was the custom, the studies from life are more sensitive, usually more linear, and seem surprisingly soon to explore the idea of surface planes which was later to become such an issue, in the form of Cubism, for the mature Picasso (see *Croquis diversos*, fig.5.6).

He was still incorrigibly improving his schoolbooks with sketches of comic figures or bizarre events, continuing his own quirkish tradition. To amuse friends and relatives he portrayed local characters and their activities, often with quite savage humour. But during 1894 these largely gave way to studies on drawing-paper which, while perpetuating many of the old themes, began to exploit more consciously the teachings of the school and of his father.

Most importantly, he broadened his outlook by tackling studies of rural landscapes; these reveal more than anything else at this time the acceleration in his acquisition of skills. He learned to manipulate composition; in *Alquería* (fig.5.7) the plough links the foreground earth-mounds to the house, doorway and figure. Interior details are effectively suggested by subtle tonal variations; different textures of line convey the nature of the object-materials they delineate: these are subtle tricks which depend for their success upon at least an intuitive awareness of the power and integrity of the medium in any image. *Tarde en el campo* is a pencil sketch of figures under trees near a farm, reminiscent of compositions ten years earlier by the Post-Impressionist painter Georges Seurat (although Pablo Ruiz could not then have seen them). No doubt encouraged by his father, he made use of his new learning from the life room, to execute a number of systematic portrait studies.

The child's creative activity at this time could have been stimulated by an adverse emotional experience (as Freudian theory proposed) during the year following his thirteenth birthday. The year 1895 began traumatically for him with the death of his much-loved

while his interest in the inanimate remained (at this time) comparatively slight. He continued to adorn his textbook margins with a variety of Roman and other soldiers, portraits (including some animal ones), the occasional odd structural image (as though he were plotting a piece of woodwork), some lively caricatures, heads (some bearded or turbaned, some smoking), pistols and rifles, flowers, tubes of paint, birds and copulating donkeys.

The treatment of these images is diverse: some are naive and slight, while others show how much he had already learned of what a pencil or a pen could be made to do. Some illustrate handwritten journals which were made to amuse or to impress his wealthy uncle and also to let people know in Málaga what life was allegedly like in La Coruña. Richardson is suspicious about the differences of quality between the naive and the academic work of this time.[15] But this phenomenon in children may signal an adaptive attitude where testing different modes of drawing

5.7 Pablo Ruiz Picasso, *Alquería* (MBP 111.399), 1894
(age 13); © Succession Picasso/DACS 2000

sister Conchita; his work became even more prolific. It seems unlikely that the artistic fervour which had propelled him thus far could ever have been crushed in respect of the pact which he claimed to have made with God to give up painting if his sister could live. The survival of his passion, seemingly at the expense of her life, could have filled him with guilt. But his discomfort might have been even greater had she lived and he had proved unable to honour the unwise bargain. In the event, he was to join the La Llotja art school in Barcelona in September 1895, soon after his father had obtained a better post there.

At this time his father is said to have handed over his own brushes to his son in a relinquishing gesture. If true, this may have been merely symbolic or it could have been a distortion of events by Picasso himself, realising retrospectively the importance of his transition from artist's son to independent student for both of them. It does also beg the question as to whether Pablo Ruiz's work at this time might have justified

such a gesture, and there is little doubt on several counts that it would have done so. Collectively his work shows an insatiable curiosity and all the obsessional characteristics of the committed, albeit still very uneven, young artist. In terms of subject-matter it probes in several directions, on the one hand grasping at the traditional and the formal through intense observation and recording by conventional techniques, and on the other splendidly curious in imaginative as well as observational ways.

Picasso's biographers portray a fairly arrogant young man at this stage, impatient to be admitted to the Barcelona school, something of a braggart about his past achievements and contemptuous of the ability of La Llotja to do much for him. In fact, its greatest service would not be in the form of its teaching, which was uninspired, but in providing him with innumerable, though mostly male, life models. In the light of his attainments to that date, it is not difficult to see some justification for his arrogance and impatience.

5.8 Pablo Ruiz Picasso, *Copia de 'El bufón calabacillas' de Velázquez* (MBP 111.170R), 1895 (age 14); © Succession Picasso/DACS 2000

He was already mature enough as an artist to realize what in later life he believed, that 'What is taught in the Ecoles des Beaux Arts has only to do with craft and not with painting',[17] which anyway was precisely what he ultimately argued to be their most useful role.

In La Coruña he had engaged in a fair amount of copying, not only from drawings of the Antique but also from the paintings of minor Spanish artists that were available to him. While on a brief visit to the Prado in Madrid (en route for a family vacation in Málaga), he encountered for the first time the original works of great artists, strengthening his understanding of portraiture with some studies from Velázquez (fig. 5.8). Later in Barcelona he had additional reason to copy from the Prado's collections, because there was a continuing absence of female models in the art school.

Perhaps because of the decline and eventual loss of one sister and a consequent deepening family awareness, there was an increase in family studies, of the dying Conchita as well as of Lola and his parents. He could already obtain sophisticated likenesses and understood the use in them of chiaroscuro; his family portraits were supplemented by many other studies of people generally. Richardson argues that it is 'the fervour and urgency' of these works that is significant and that the evident erratic struggle was a struggle to go beyond and above his father's 'lack of accomplishment'.[18] When at this time the increasingly independent thirteen-year-old Pablo Ruiz ventured to display a couple of oil portraits in a local shop-window, they attracted a favourable and predictive review in the local press, as Richardson records.[19] But his use of colour was still subdued by the Spanish tradition and teaching, with only occasional forays into a higher key than was customary.

During the family's stay in Málaga, his uncle Salvador provided him with a model, an old fisherman who posed for him on several occasions, both clothed and nude. The necessity to please Salvador tended to result in the creation of some of the boy's most conventional and least individual works. Richardson calls them 'feeble' and thinks that Pablo Ruiz was in a holiday mood,[20] but they are nonetheless very strong and characterful statements, excellent for any boy who was not Picasso. Some drawings, directly observed or remembered, are mild caricatures of people in the streets (*Una familia paseando*). One multiple sketch, *El Panteón*, in which he interwove the Venus de Milo with various cupids, a colonnaded façade, a portrait of Velázquez and one of Cervantes holding a copy of his *Don Quijote*, could be said to reveal a growing awareness of links between literature, architecture and visual art.

With or without the help of his Barcelona teachers, Picasso's studies of this time were strikingly accomplished and show the artist's conviction of the need to study drawing as a craft. He had discovered how to turn his flat paper surface into an arena for space and shadow, where form gleams, poised in front of darkness; nude studies show the human body as a dynamic force in space (a discovery of major significance for his mature work as a painter). Sometimes these latter studies are conventionally rich in observed detail, as in the overworked examination drawing, *Hombre desnudo*, done for entry to La Llotja; sometimes they acquired a quite different character when circumstances provided the necessary freedom to explore alternatives. He worked again, and more determinedly, on the idea of surface planes in *Estudio de desnudo masculino* (fig.5.9); another drawing indicates that he was testing the implications of informal perspective and implied movement on a drawing of the human torso.

The mature Picasso was essentially an artist of

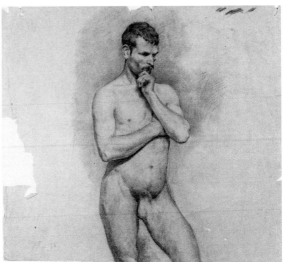

5.10 Pablo Ruiz Picasso, *Academia del natural* (MBP 110.881), 1895–96 (age 14–15); © Succession Picasso/DACS 2000

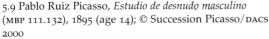

5.9 Pablo Ruiz Picasso, *Estudio de desnudo masculino* (MBP 111.132), 1895 (age 14); © Succession Picasso/DACS 2000

flexibility; nothing occurred to him that could not be manipulated, reinterpreted, envisaged in other forms or contexts. By the time he was thirteen he had already realized that tradition could be a straitjacket and that techniques could be constantly varied. He knew how to masquerade as different kinds of artist, to make a drawing linearly dynamic, tonally mysterious, grotesquely funny or respectably traditional. The peak of his formal performance in this period is evidenced in the impressive life drawing of a nude male, *Academia del natural* (fig.5.10) placed in time either just before or soon after his fourteenth birthday. But important clues to his attitude and hints for his future are to be found in his eclectic and spontaneous gathering of other material: soldiers, animals, boats and seascapes, flowers, architecture and small compositions, together with his varied experimentation with media, mainly pencil, pen and oils, as well as with treatment and composition.

He was being rigorously disciplined as an artist rather than being awakened as one, but (and in contrast with his retrospective view of himself) the personal modes and interests were still present in the background. He was becoming highly experienced in the medium of oils and one portrait in particular, *La muchacha de los pies descalzos* (fig.5.11), with undertones of Murillo, which he undertook in 1895, demonstrates this latent individualism and free spirit more than words can say. It is an uncompromising work, markedly different in the presentation of the figure, free use of colour and loose application of paint from the more conventional and painstaking techniques into which he was being inducted all the time. Of this remarkable painting, which seems defiantly to mark a key moment in the development of Picasso as an autonomous artist, Vallentin reasonably suggests that 'clearly his eyes understood more than his brain could assimilate'.[21]

The achievements of 1895, following upon his four-

5.11 Pablo Ruiz Picasso, *La muchacha de los pies descalzos*
(MP 2), 1895 (age 14); © Succession Picasso/DACS 2000

5.12 Pablo Ruiz Picasso, *La procesión* (MBP 110.646),
1895–96 (age 14–15); © Succession Picasso/DACS 2000

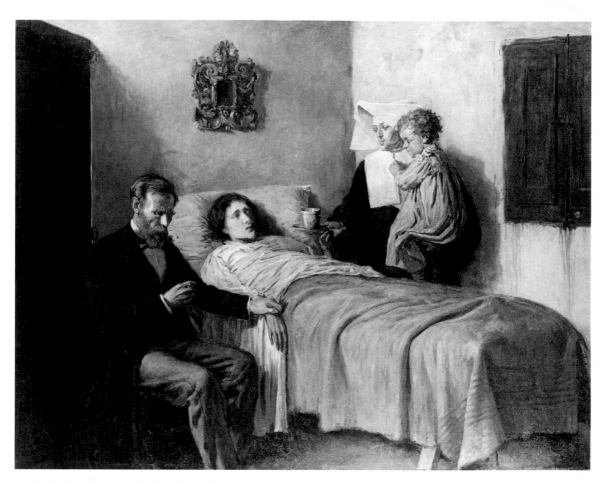

5.16 Pablo Ruiz Picasso, *Ciencia y Caridad* (MBP 110.046),
1897 (age 16); © Succession Picasso/DACS 2000

5.17 Pablo Ruiz Picasso, *Mujer en azul*, Madrid 1901
(age 19); © Succession Picasso/DACS 2000

5.18 Pablo Ruiz Picasso, *Caricaturas de 'Decadentes'*
(MBP 110.297R) (age 17–18); © Succession Picasso/
DACS 2000

would arrive in Paris after further studies in Barcelona
and Madrid. In those four years he would have
replicated the achievements of *Primera Comunión*
numerous times. The several preliminary studies for
another big opus, *Ciencia y Caridad* (fig.5.16), a Gold
Medal winner at the Málaga Provincial Exhibition in
that year, completed when he was fifteen and a half,
show the tenacity and professionalism which he could
by then employ, as do the many other smaller spontaneous works.

Picasso never ceased to copy from the works of
artists he admired, including El Greco, Velázquez and
especially Goya, the latter no doubt providing new
insight into a more idiosyncratic view of art. Some
drawings made before he was eighteen evoke the style
of Toulouse-Lautrec, for example in *Muchacha de Perfil*,
a series which eventually culminated in the mag-

nificent portrait *Mujer en azul* (fig.5.17). Ostensibly his
subject-matter changed very little in the years from
fifteen to nineteen; the principal and crucial difference
is in a developing and triumphant energy and freedom. In drawings and caricatures of 'Decadentes'
(fig.5.18), a blasphemous theme according to Richardson, the dominant foreground figure is paralleled with
a loosely but vigorously drawn repetition, as though
exploring the breaking up of the form and its linear
consequences.[22]

Without the startling developments of the six years
prior to age fifteen and his reaction to the pressures
put upon him during those years, the outcome for
Picasso as an artist might have been very different. So
it is worth taking a closer look at some of the circumstances underpinning as well as immediately prior to
this accelerative period.

Richardson suggests that Málaga was a 'stagnant' place and Picasso's father a 'complacent victim' of its nature; 'the son was therefore all the more eager to disavow this dismal heritage'.[23] One can see that Picasso as a boy may have been driven to escape from his father's influence in order to establish his own individuality. But as father to such a child, Don José, the accredited if minor-talented professor of painting, was nevertheless extremely useful in directing all his teaching and artistic skills towards this remarkable pupil, even though it is clear that the pressure he applied from the beginning to his son carried disadvantages.

Don José Ruiz ('the pigeon painter')[24] appears to have been a dedicated if pedantic artist whose work was more respected then admired (Picasso's mature dismissal of his father as a painter of 'dining-room pictures' is oft-quoted). As a professional teacher, it would have been only natural for him to seize upon any inclination towards drawing which his son displayed and to begin to exert his own influence upon it. The enduring phenomena of his subject-matter (such as the doves and pigeons) are part of the evidence of that. Although Don José is said to have been only 'a modest craftsman',[25] he also impressed the child with his transforming activities, such as re-dressing plaster images with paint and crystal tears,[26] another formative experience for Picasso.

Vallentin possibly underestimates Picasso's father, given the undoubted persistence of his teaching, describing 'a contemplative man, averse to struggle and easily discouraged'.[27] But whatever he meant to achieve, he inadvertently performed the same essentially valuable role later ascribed by Richardson to Fernande Olivier, one of Picasso's later mistresses, of being 'the grit that created the pearl in the oyster'.[28] Walther describes a similar process: 'Though it may seem astonishing or paradoxical, the fact is that Picasso did not become Picasso under the influence of progressive ideas but because an old-fashioned milieu was imposing superannuated notions on him.'[29] Some argue that his desire to escape from his father's personality and influence was epitomized in his later decision to drop his father's name, Ruiz, in favour of his mother's. But in doing that, he was following a Spanish convention as well as taking the name that had greater local cachet.

The family household itself may have been difficult to inhabit. Some say that Pablo Ruiz's mother was 'sickly, wilful, sluggish and dominating',[30] or that she dominated through her own weaknesses.[31] There is much agreement that the relationship between mother and son was uneasy; they were too much alike. Gedo believes that they had in common an 'extreme vulnerability in self-esteem',[32] which may account both for

the way she appears to have underrated his potential and also for the aggressive behaviour which he indulged in as a child.

Picasso later believed that she had recognized his exceptionality early on, but Doña Maria seems mainly to have been apprehensive about his behaviour and the personality resonant in his attractive but piercing eyes. It may only have been in later years that she revealed the sense of humour which (in his own way) her son may have owed to her.[33] Given that particular trait, it seems less likely that she was as ineffectual in the family home as some writers depict. Pablo Ruiz may have had to contend with two demanding parents.

He had also to establish his position as the only male child in a household of largely female relatives, including several aunts as well as his sisters. Some biographers see this as an overwhelming situation for him, others as one in which he easily thrived because he knew how to manipulate it; Richardson argues that the child became fractious but also devious – both characteristics that are arguably apparent later in the mature adult.[34]

Drawing was clearly the most powerful means open to him by which to attract attention. From the beginning he used it even to acquire things such as food (he drew what he wanted to eat) and to reveal himself as an individual, different and with different skills from others around him. He was only three when his sister Lola was born and the event appears to have been traumatic, so that his father found it necessary to distract him by giving him drawing tasks, as we have seen; no doubt pleased to have captured attention, he would have found he could retain it by continuing to draw.

It is not just what happens to a child that is significant but also (and more importantly) what the child perceives *about himself* in relation to the domestic, social and imaginative worlds which form his experience of life. And (it is said) Pablo Ruiz had experienced a revelation of a kind, of an almost magical nature, when at three years of age he confused the celebrations for the ceremonial return of King Don Alfonso to Málaga with preparations for the return of the painter Don Antonio, whom he knew his father much admired. In his mind the status of the artist assumed proportions of exceptional grandeur and this contributed to the early development of his ambition; it may be true that, as Stassinopoulos-Huffington says, 'a momentous association was made at that moment in the mind of the three-year old between painting and glory'.[35]

No one can know whether such a vision of the glory of being an artist was actually necessary as a stimulus to someone such as Picasso. Given what we additionally know of his background and personality, it seems merely incidental, although trivial incidents may sometimes have long-term consequences. There may have been inherited preconditions which determined his future; genetic arguments could be constructed from the incidence of artists in his family. Recent ancestors had been artists and his grandfather was a good musician who also practised drawing; some of Don José's brothers studied painting or became connoisseurs of art; in general terms the family into which Pablo Ruiz was born was artistically inclined. But his own disposition may have been due less to inheritance than to example and was in any case an obsession of quite a different order.

Another argument focuses on physical causes; where Don José was comparatively tall and distinguished in a way Spaniards saw as looking 'English', his son was dark and short. Perhaps this might have been a factor in generating an exceptional competitive initiative; but apart from the unreliability of the theory, it is difficult to see why a boy who looked like others around him and was not, before adolescence at least, all that much shorter than others, would be so affected.

No one has speculated very much on the implications of the child's behaviour, although there is a general consensus that Picasso as a child had some educational, emotional and social difficulties. Several biographers refer to learning difficulties which were evident during his first years at school; he was unusually slow in learning to read and write. Picasso himself referred to these difficulties in support of his arguments that growing up and becoming a painter had been at times particularly difficult.

Some judge the learning block to have been quite severe, particularly but not only in mathematics; paradoxically his phobic responses included obsessions with numbers involving 'repeated chanting of the time'. Gedo suggests that 'his mathematical learning block was aggravated by his inability to assume the abstract attitude'.[36] Put another way, this might mean that he could not easily conceptualize from sensory experience.

There were other behavioural problems stemming, some would say, from his family life. According to Gedo, 'an unusual dependence on partnerships' meant that:

By the time he had reached school age, Pablo Ruiz would become quite disorganised whenever he had to separate from his family, especially his empathetic father. His entry into first grade was traumatic for the future artist, who reacted with pervasive, agitated emotional paralysis which was to recur throughout his life whenever a crucial relationship disintegrated or was interrupted by external events and he found himself alone.[37]

Gedo records how the child, with a 'severe school phobia', had to be dragged to school, made 'noisy, terrible scenes', feigned illness and needed a guarantee of his father's return such as the promise of paint brushes or a pigeon.[38] Richardson is cynical about the accuracy of some of these descriptions (those that derive from the artist's own accounts), believing that the mature Picasso was extending the view of himself as a genius emerging with struggle against extreme disadvantages; he believes that a highly intelligent individual such as the child Picasso undoubtedly was, would have been unlikely to encounter difficulties with language and expression.[39] But such paradoxical phenomena are by no means unknown.

When Picasso's friend Pallares was an old man, he described Pablo Ruiz at the age of fourteen, as he had observed him in the La Llotja art school. Pallares remembers that, although the younger boy seemed not to listen, he was quicker than anyone to learn and understand; Pallares describes how he 'absorbed things in the blink of an eye and remembered them months later'.[40]

Collectively, these descriptions do not add up to a total account of the early behaviour of those now commonly classified as autistic, but they do match it in a surprising number of respects. The symptoms of such a condition, which vary much in intensity between individuals affected by it, include difficulties with spoken or written language, in concept-formation, in some physical activities and social situations, as well as obsessive behaviours or interests. Common obsessions include the mathematical, the musical and the visually artistic. Obsessive behaviour may be unhelpfully repetitive but sometimes reveals startling competencies, such as unusual drawing fluency. Remarkable memory feats, often from apparently fleeting observations, are common to many such individuals. Picasso, as a child, exhibited some of these phenomena, though he was far from actually being autistic. Along with some other artists with similar behavioural histories he may have possessed or rapidly developed a condition, signalled by some of these phenomena, favouring sensory and imaginative expression as a positive compelling reaction to pressures he experienced.

Genetic, experiential and physical causes for the condition of autism have all been advanced. Among the latter of these, birth trauma of a physical nature is suggested. In this context, the events of Picasso's birth might be thought significant. It is said that he was stillborn but that his breathing was successfully stimulated by the application to his nostrils of his uncle's cigarsmoke.[41] But to accept deterministically birth-accident as an explanation for artistic achievement leaves the emergence of some artists at least as apparently open entirely to chance.

The truth may be more complex. In Picasso's case, all the many circumstances of his earliest years – the opportunities, anxieties and pressures of family and school life – seem likely to have played their part in developing his obsession. If his early behaviour indicates a condition (however acquired) favouring the development of artistic fluency, it may have combined with his other experiences dynamically to fuel the obsession, but might not in itself have guaranteed such a development.

A way of contemplating modern art is to say that it represents a powerful search through perceptions for abstractions. In that view, Picasso's early and continuing obsession with drawing and painting is deeply understandable in him. The circumstances of his childhood and the pressures on his developing personality could be supposed to have ignited a bonfire of creative ambition, accounting for his spectacular development between nine and fifteen years, with its unique longer-term consequences for the history of art.

6

A savage and gentle passion:
Michael Rothenstein (1908–1993)

I think what I did quite unconsciously as a child is in many ways like the things I do now: I work to get the optimum sort of excitement out of the colour, the angles or the drawing.

Michael Rothenstein, in an interview with the author, October 1988

Michael Rothenstein's early years were lived in a generally supportive and indulgent environment, apparently lacking in the traumatic familial or educational circumstances which many other young artists have had to surmount. The collection of his consistently vigorous and evocative drawings from those years is extensive.[1] They are imbued with energy and obsessive ideas, preoccupied with techniques avidly explored, with the power inherent in the materials and passion for the images themselves.

He was an artist from a family of artists, writers on the arts and arts administrators. His father was the painter William Rothenstein and his mother the actress Alice Knewstub. One could argue that there was some degree of inevitability in the forming of his own career. At least from the age of four, he drew prolifically. In his eighties and right up to the time of his death (he died sitting beside his beloved 'Columbian' printing press), he was still prolifically active, exhibiting constantly in Britain and overseas, revered as an artist, teacher and British Royal Academician (see *The Blue House*, fig.6.1).

The intervening years had seen him emerge as the most influential and innovative printmaker in Britain; the work and teaching of British art colleges in the 1960s were much influenced by his lead in the use of 'found' materials for an open-block method of printing, and in the process of caustic etching of lino. Some of his influence on printmaking and on its imagery also permeated into British schools. Invited to exhibit and to lecture many times in the United States, Canada, Italy, Norway and other American, European and African venues, he acquired a high international profile.

Born in London in 1908, for the first four years of

his life his family resided in the hilly and fashionable Hampstead district; their house had extensive views across London. He could always recall its fine details and some incidents in it, some real and some arising from his always active imagination.[2]

He could never remember a time when he was not drawing, but, since few of the works were ever dated, it is a matter of judgement whether there are drawings in the collection which survive from these first few years. Some certainly display the manipulative inexperience and the conceptual and visual naivety associated with the drawing of children at around three years. But in these sometimes half-finished drawings, awkward angular lines still convey, in their diagrammatic, often dynamic and occasionally humorous modes, crude human forms, fish or small sparrow-like creatures duelling with swords or handguns (see *Many figures*, fig.6.2). Most of the interest in nature, comedy, aggression and anthropomorphism that was to characterize the drawings of the next decade is already discernible.

By the time he was four years of age, the family had moved to a large stone farmhouse in Gloucestershire and, as he later put it, 'some element of observation entered in' to the drawings he was making. Behind the house was a somnolent undulating landscape of fields and hills; contrastingly a railway tunnel pierced the hill directly in front of it. The latter enduringly impressed him, with its harsh and sudden noises and its magical visions of steam, speed and power, 'like some grim anthropomorphic riddle' as he expressed it later.[3] There was a chaotic farmyard, bestrewn with barns, stables and sheds containing animals and farm equipment.

Rothenstein remembered the remoteness from other families of this stimulating but also isolated place, where he grew up safely apart from the first major European war, with his sisters as his main companions. His memories were largely idyllic; the Cotswold house

6.1 Michael Rothenstein, *The Blue House*, 1986

6.2 Michael Rothenstein, *Many figures*, 1912 (age 4)

was 'in a marvellous valley. You could walk out in the fields on a summer day and the chorus of birds and grasshoppers was just symphonic … I would get drunk with the light or butterflies flying round a bush … wonderful pools between the locks – places of such excitement and mystery – hanging woods, and water-lilies.'[4] This was a time without cars, radio or television, with the steam railway as the major image of distance transport and the pony trap or bicycle for local journeys. The children found their entertainment in the locality and in nature. A nearby canal, full of water snakes and minnows, was a constant source of interest: 'there were a couple of streams and places where the water connected in an old stone trough where cows used to drink. Even on a winter's day, there was this wonderful, green, pristine luminosity of summer.'[5] Judging by the many affectionate annotated caricatures which Rothenstein later drew of members of his family, this childhood country life forged strong family feeling in him. The children shared a children's world of exploration and games, but also participated

in adult events with their parents. His sisters drew, but less passionately, and his elder brother's drawings were more inhibited; the latter always 'used a ruler', whereas Michael's style was adaptive, flexible and free.

Some of his first drawings were done with chalks ('Yes, I loved those pastels I had, you know, mauve and pink, stroking the paper with those wonderful powdery colours, an incredible delight');[6] he felt that he had always been interested in the characteristics of the medium, and how it determined the nature of the drawings. A particular delight had been his first watercolour box, received at five or six years, 'one of those wonderful black japanned boxes with little white china cups of colour'.[7] He quickly discovered how the medium could be rendered soft and ethereal or rich and vibrant. What happened to the colours as he worked often suggested the ideas, a first fresh colour providing a vivid flame, for instance, against a sombre background from the progressive dirtying of tints on the palette. The materials were both stimulating and inspiring.

6.3 Michael Rothenstein, *Birds, bees and butterflies*, 1913
(age 5)

When Michael was about six years of age, he and his sisters captured newts, minnows and sticklebacks from the canal and local ponds with their fishing nets and set up an aquarium at home in a glass tank. Here they studied these fascinating little creatures and drew them frequently, often from memory. This subject-matter, together with other natural phenomena – the lilies, the butterflies and the farmyard animals (including horses and cockerels) – was to re-emerge at intervals throughout his entire life as an artist. Michael made deliciously watery colour studies and some later pencil drawings of fish and insects (see *Birds, bees and butterflies*, fig.6.3). He gave some as gifts to his mother, embellished with kisses and inscribed 'from her own little boy'; at this time his father often seemed 'remote, preoccupied, always writing letters'.[8] In the background there were always narrative drawings; one lively drawing shows lions and tigers hiding in the forest from the poised arrows of advancing Indians. The ability to compose the elements of a narrative in this way was something that Michael had learned unusually quickly.

The focus on the farmyard extended to farm and other machinery, exploring form and function with a mechanical sensitivity that seems at first quite different from his interest in nature. Tractor wheels, telephone wires, chimneys and the metal cladding of machinery caught his attention. The engine and railway drawings are recurrent throughout his childhood and, since the trains passed so close to the house, it is not surprising that Magritte-like engines and tunnels feature in these functional studies, carrying their own physical and sexual symbolism, as Rothenstein recognized retrospectively:

the breast-like swelling of the dome; the dark phallus of the funnel, spouting furious smoke clouds; the bunched fists of the buffers out in front. And finally the driver and stoker on the footplate; black twins, you might think, born of the scarlet hell-womb of the furnace mouth. In some of the drawings these two figures have been wildly contorted, as if enraged or maddened by the heat.[9]

Numerous drawings of engines and carriages survive, at first mere diagrams, then bizarre combinations

6.4 Michael Rothenstein, *Armoured figure*, c.1915–16 (age 7–8)

of machine and operator and eventually expressions of the full force of puffing steam and racing, clanking wheels. Preoccupied with the idea of protectively clad objects, whether trains or shellfish ('I used to love shrimps, the way they curl up and their little legs come out'), he completed a number of drawings of armoured figures (at around eight or nine years) with an engineer's attention to the shaping of the metal, its articulations and its fastenings (see fig.6.4). He began linking the inanimate with the animate, combining knowledge with imagination by inventing armoured beasts. In these drawings it is clear that to him surfaces were sensual things and also, as he later commented, 'When you draw that, you know there's a body underneath that has three-dimensionality.'[10]

Model soldiers were given to him by an uncle. German in origin, boxed, embossed and boldly coloured, they invited constant rearrangement on a simulated battlefield, provoking drawings of imagined military scenes and stories, in which they featured in all the glory of their plumed helmets and striped trousers. Some of these characters are not far away from the profile drawings of birds in their buttoned coats which are among Michael's first-known sketches. The earlier drawings are birds made human (see fig.6.5); the later ones are humans given the plumage of birds.

Another equally formative subject came from a wonderful collection of Rajput miniatures which Michael's father had acquired. These the boy found fascinating, not only for their intricacy of detail but also for their cultural strangeness; he particularly remembered how some of the aristocratic figures were portrayed with green or purple faces. He recreated many from memory, with as much interest in the character of the image as in its detail (see *Birds on leafy branches*, pl.v).

Although the Gloucestershire house was isolated (not unusually so by the standards of the time, of course), it was not without its literary and social riches, including a substantial collection of art books owned by his father. Michael was impressed by some Uccello paintings, no doubt particularly the military action subjects. He remembered learning from Greek sculpture the idea that there is a ledge between the brow and the beginning of the nose. He collected cigarette cards, too, which provided exciting information about uniforms; there was the customary selection of books of fable and fantasy, from *The Arabian Nights* to *Struwwelpeter*. From newspapers he discovered the distant contemporary world of conflict at sea; he drew and painted his own versions of firing ships and ships on fire (for example *Sea battle*, fig.6.6). Few as these sources may have been, they fuelled his imagination with the information they provided about the world beyond Gloucestershire.

His father also had plenty of stimulating and eminent friends, especially poets and painters, who were frequent visitors to the house. Bryan Robertson (in an obituary for the *Independent* newspaper, 9 July 1993) noted that:

As a child and as a young man, he [Rothenstein] enjoyed the not affluent but comfortable style of an artist's household in which Wyndham Lewis, Edward Burra, Stanley Spencer, David Jones, Edwin Lutyens or the young Henry Moore were received and he often rubbed shoulders at supper or tea parties with Walter de la Mare, Barnett Freedman or Robert Graves.[11]

In his own memories of those times, Rothenstein perceived two disparate existences for the children of the house, one in which they led a totally undisciplined life in the woods and fields and in their fantasy activi-

6.5 Michael Rothenstein, *Helmeted birds*, c.1913 (age 5)

ties and the other in which their residence was a kind of 'Cotswold Camelot', as he spoke of it, a rich exotic upper layer of social contact. Max Beerbohm and Bernard Shaw were particular memories for him; he did not meet Edward Burra until he was fifteen and then not initially at home. The children were encouraged to sing and otherwise exhibit their talents for visitors; Rothenstein remembered himself behaving like 'the prize genius' as he enjoyed showing off his drawing prowess.

Although he was much affected by visual information from books and paintings, textual and literary material were not so important to him. He recalled how he was slow in learning to read; according to him it was not until he was nine years of age that he conquered this initial disability; inscriptions on some of the drawings do not entirely confirm this. But he described his attempts at writing before then as 'pretty primitive'and felt that as a young child he had lived much more with images than with words.[12]

He drew when excited, frustrated, angry, afraid, to act out a fantasy or to display the brilliance he knew was noticed, but in an intense and not merely casual way. It is therefore not surprising that implicit action is frequently more important than any other aspect in many of his drawings. Birds are more often shown in flight or spreading their wings than stationary. Soldiers march or fight (people batter each other generally!) and others dance, run, fly or throw things. It is arguable that such intense activity may have been instrumental in the development of emotional maturity.

In these childhood years (less apparent in adolescence), there was a contrast between the gentle observations of rural detail in some drawings and the astonishingly cruel portrayals of physical violence in others. Mel Gooding explained this paradox of Rothenstein's childhood as 'Visions of paradise, intimations of hell; the true reality of the world we inherit is contained in those dynamic oppositions.'[13] Rothenstein saw himself as having been a 'wild but gentle' child, though wild only in the sense of being undisciplined, and he marvelled retrospectively at his own drawn expressions of fiendish aggression.[14] The shyness and unease which beset him for some time as an adult were conditions which began in childhood and which provoked in this child some compensatory action through drawing. On one such drawing, of a seated human figure that is bloody from an axe which has sliced

6.6 Michael Rothenstein, *Sea battle*, c.1914–16 (age 6–8)

through his head (fig.6.7), Rothenstein was able to be quite specific as to his motivation at the time:

If a man had come to the house with a dark moustache, if he was an officer or something, I always found those figures very intimidating and would have thoroughly enjoyed intimidating them in my drawings. That's a wood axe that has entered his head, we had those axes in the shed, my delight was in getting the other half [of the head], that red silhouette. He's cut down to his chest and there's the neck and the chin and the silhouette of the head. [The writing] places the drawing later [than six years]. [With] most figures [drawn] in action there would be combat and an assailant, but this is pure concept and there's no assailant. I think I was so delighted by the idea, I didn't need an assailant. The artist was the assailant.[15]

These malevolent images placated the dark side of an otherwise agreeable nature or were part of 'a constructive retreat into drawing and painting [which] provided refuge or at least a relief from the profound shyness and nervousness', as Robertson suggests.[16] But many of Michael's early drawings (often signed 'Billy', the name by which his family knew him until he was sixteen) are resplendent with the imaginative logic of the hypothesis, not only when expressing violence. His soldiers march in multiples, divested of their originally leaden rigidity (see fig.6.8); the observed birds, fish and cockerels are transformed into characters, mysteriously masked or anthropomorphically dressed. He 'created' mythical islands by mapping them. Studies of insects have an ambiguity of scale and detail which leaves their nature as either small friendly beasts or menacing giants undetermined.

The drawings of this period are very direct, suggesting that in the act of drawing, at least, Michael was self-confident, unhampered at that time either by artistic convention or by the attitudes of other children. His earliest drawings had been full of exuberant whirling lines and geometric forms used for speedy effect; sometimes a continuous line would convey the running legs of his figures or the entire body of a dog. Later drawings exploited these earliest techniques in new contexts; thus the succession of curving lines used to describe the plated body of an insect seems inherited from much earlier drawings as well as also being used to convey the concertina'd sleeves of figures with arms upraised.

This adaptive fluency seems to have led easily to comic expression. The line between aggression and humour is a thin one; some of the most horrific of

6.9 Michael Rothenstein, *Bird soldier*, 1915–17 (age 7–9)

drawings; his writing had improved. Observations he had first made in Gloucestershire were recycled as he sophisticated earlier skeletal and armoured animal figures. But the technique had changed; contours are flowing and even; bone-like features merge with muscular ones and there is a point where they begin to seem more decorative. The simpler profiled portrayal of such fantasy creatures resembling fish, insects or dragons is eventually discarded as the intention is no longer to show a static diagrammatic posture but to suggest movement and menace. These particular drawings hint at the violence and aggression of earlier, more child-like pieces, without the horror or even the humour of them.

During the years of Michael's early adolescence,

from 1920 to 1924, his sister Rachel was ill for long periods and in a convalescent home some distance away. His attachment to her had always been strong and he comforted himself as well as amusing her by a constant stream of illustrated letters (see *Wembley Funfair*, fig.6.10). Contemplating these years later, he seemed anxious about his unsympathetic portrayals of people, particularly of his elder sister Betty. Some are certainly unflattering, but he gave much the same treatment to all.

Adept at using a pen, his ink lines were at this stage firm and confident if not yet intentionally aesthetic beyond their illustrative purpose. From these sketches, particularly prolific in his fifteenth and sixteenth years, Rachel in her bed would have learned how their father

Here is a drawing of a dreadful machine of torture that I went on at Wembley. The worst of it is that all the people standing round laugh so much.) ! ! ! * !

6.10 Michael Rothenstein, *Wembley Funfair*, c.1924 (age 16)

6.11 Michael Rothenstein, *Father playing tennis at Ainslie Gardens*, c.1923–24 (age 15–16)

6.12 Michael Rothenstein, *Betty's move*, c.1923–24 (age 15–16)

looked, according to Michael's satirical view of him, diving for a ball on the tennis court; these drawings owe much to the conventions of the comic-book but are also effective as caricature portraits (fig.6.11). She would be able to see her sister collecting specimens for her aquarium, changing the water in it and delighting in its size and wriggling contents (see *Betty's move*, fig.6.12). She could enjoy, through one of Michael's more gestural drawings, the hectic experience of attending a crowded private view at the Royal Academy in London. And she could anticipate the welcome she would eventually receive on her return home from two contrasting comic sketches; in one, a stylish but economically drawn image shows the crowds cheering behind a barrier as her limousine appears; in another much racier and more grotesque drawing, she is being carried down the street on a stretcher by two scruffy workmen.

A significant drawing from the same time shows Michael himself walking down a bill-posted street, identifying himself as an artist by the clutch of brushes in his hand, as a defiant adolescent by the name over the grocer's shop ('B. Rotten, Family Stores') and as a cheerfully cynical brother by the legend on the cinema poster: 'A stupendouse [sic] film, *Why Girls Marry*, starring Betty Rothenstein and Harry Moore' (fig.6.13).

There is great strength and style in all these works as well as an obvious need to assert (largely by gentle mockery) his own personality against family pressures or anything which he perceived as constraining ('When I got into my teens, I began to build a wall, because I wanted to keep my distance: I felt so different').[19] Curiously, his choice of favourite images at this time for his own room included one closely echoing the violent subjects of his childhood years. It was a reproduction of a Mantegna in which a prostrate saint awaits execution by a blow to the skull from a wooden mallet. The ferocity of the executioner, the indifference of the onlooking figures and the cultivated detachment of the

victim were a subject of wonder much remarked upon in discussions with the painter Stanley Spencer on several of his visits.[20]

By mid-adolescence, pen was largely superseding pencil and Michael was also trying out the effects of quill pens; pen lines sweep confidently through the images and across pages. Character and caricature grew in authority; with drawing, he amplified the personalities of many people he met. He also speculated on the possible futures of those he knew well: his father if he should over-eat; Betty having perhaps become a prestigious lecturer (this drawing, unusually for this period is made atmospheric by the use of tone) or alternatively the harassed mother of several children; the growth of his friend Marvin's already large nose; or himself as an artist in five, ten and in twenty years' time and at eighty 'if fate be kind'.

This visual autobiography leaves no doubt of the author's early commitment to becoming an artist. Inverting time, he also considered his own past in the

6.13 Michael Rothenstein, *Why Girls Marry*, c.1923–24
(age 15)

6.14 Michael Rothenstein, *Self-portrait with large drawing*, c.1923–24 (age 15–16)

6.15 Michael Rothenstein, *Betty, Frank Medley and Spear*, c.1925 (age 16–17)

form of the occasion of his birth and as a child in his pram, already sketching. He made a sketch from memory of his first visit as a child to the National Gallery; the notes added years later tell how he remembered the occasion: he had stared at Titian's *Bacchus and Ariadne* for over twenty minutes and then rushed home to try to recreate a part of it in watercolour, 'a peep of blue sea with a cliff with a tree growing on top'.[21]

Much of this confident attitude will have come from his first phase of tuition as an art student. At fourteen years of age he had begun to study at the School of Art and Woodcarving in South Kensington, because 'my father had rather Pre-Raphaelite ideas, that artists should be craftspeople before being free creative painters'.[22] Michael's interest in using tools himself was slight, although he was later to get others to use them on his behalf. During this time he found himself

working beside Edward Burra, who later became a friend and in due course an eminent painter. They studied watercolour together, 'but I used more gouache', said Rothenstein, believing that Burra had little direct influence on him.[23] After a year, in 1923 when he was still only fifteen, Michael transferred to the Central School of Art in London.

In contemporary comic sketches, he depicts himself as an exuberant, unruly but dedicated student and proud enough of the first down on his chin to feature it in self-portraits. Many of these witty sketches portray the problems that a new art student has to face, such as having to work speedily from great inspiration and whether consequent drawings were therefore carelessly bad, or the practical difficulty of working on a very large surface (see *Self-portrait with large drawing*, fig.6.14). Although he had, by his own efforts, been well prepared for his art-studentship, he may have

6.16 Michael Rothenstein, *Party*, c.1924 (age 16)

been initially daunted. His father had taken him on many sketching expeditions and imbued in him not only a passion for art but also a view of the sheer length of the artistic struggle; one sketch shows father and son setting out with drawing materials, but encountering a milestone inscribed 'Truth 1000000 miles'.

Equally daunting must have been the fact that at the Central the young student felt that the teachers (and these included Bernard Meninsky) 'didn't seem to trouble much about students'.[24] His father's earlier introduction of him to the skills of artists such as Holbein and Mantegna paradoxically acted at first as a heavy constraint upon his development in drawing and painting. The family's acquaintance with Barnett Freedman provided a fortuitous liberation of his own understanding from this mental straitjacket. Freedman caused Rothenstein to think more about Cézanne: 'I felt suddenly free of the weight of that line [Mantegna's and Holbein's] of accomplishment. I saw this man who was looking at things as if nobody had ever looked at them before – the brokenness, the difficulty, that lurching into reality; it was just such a feeling of massive reality.'[25]

In the background to his academic progress, friendships and the social background to being an art student also received attention in a considerable volume of sketches; the visual appearance of each of his new friends was provocatively analysed, as in *Betty, Frank Medley and Spear* (fig.6.15); mealtimes, parties and formal dances were all gleefully recorded, still perhaps for the encouragement of convalescent Rachel, but probably also as a way of coming to terms with the intensely exciting but also demanding life he was leading (fig.6.16). In one or two revealing drawings he seems to encapsulate with humour the trepidation which stemmed no doubt from his charac-

6.17 Michael Rothenstein, *At the Central Sketch Club*, c.1924
(age 16)

teristic shyness; in one he trembles as a tutor comes to
censure him for being noisy; in another he portrays a
huge room, in the corner of which the owner cowers
on a minute bed.

Collectively, the many informal drawings of these
first years as a student convey a picture of an eager
and excited young man grasping at every new experience, even if sometimes made nervous by his own
temerity in doing so. Family support was clearly
strong and his progress to a world beyond the family
might have been more difficult without it. But the
sparky humour of the drawings was clearly supportive, enabling him to objectify a little the temporary
absence of those he most loved, the making of new
contacts, the glorious induction into the world of the
professional artist and above all the nature of the
person he was becoming. These are very personal
portrayals even when they do not directly portray the
artist. In a review of a Rothenstein exhibition which
took place in London in 1988, Waldemar Januszczak
perceptively wrote, 'The difference between Rothenstein's juvenilia and his new work is a difference of
positioning. In the childhood battle scenes he is there,
in the middle, part of the action, grabbing, flaying,

sharing. In the new pictures he is an observer, removed
from the action, watching, wishing.'[26] At around sixteen, as a young student, he was at a halfway stage in
this fascinating process, seeing himself as an instru-
ment in his own art, if not fully understanding it as
instrumental in his life or quite able to realize its
potential to transcend it (see *At the Central Sketch Club*,
fig.6.17).

The mature Rothenstein works contain strong echoes
of his childhood and adolescent drawing, though less
in the style than in the subject-matter, as when, for
example, he revisited the images from nature, the birds
and insects of his country childhood. Although they
are differently treated according to the experienced eye
of the professional and sometimes in response to the
qualities of a medium or process, they carry the same
exotic, dramatic and fundamentally exciting messages
that he always gave them. He managed to retain in
them something of his early innocence as well as what
gave them their potency: 'We paint flowers, a landscape, a face, and it's this mood of excitement, an
implied violence of structure, one is always trying to
capture.'[27]

7

The young humorist:
Gerard Hoffnung (1925–1959)

Inspiration lay for him on the borderline of fantasy, where the unpleasant can strike one as amusing and the mysterious looks almost homely.

Bruno Adler

Of all the records of an individual's early drawing development that are known to me, that of Gerard Hoffnung, which I first investigated in 1977, remains one of the most comprehensive and fascinatingly complex. A substantial historic record of the artist's early years, it gives remarkable insight into his personality and ability. It is astonishing evidence of the continuity of artistic skill and expressive interests from the earliest years to eventual professionalism.

Hoffnung became widely known in Britain during the 1950s as a broadcaster and raconteur as well as for his published illustrations caricaturing the perform-ance of music or the eccentricities of people around him. He was also identified with the uniquely comic symphony concerts for which he inveigled eminent musicians to compose or perform. Lovingly crafted by a man who was himself passionate for music, these were no acts of disrespect but rather an irreverent homage. Performed to the highest standards and full of bizarre musical references to compositions past and present, they expressed his constant delight in the comic potential of the serious.

When Hoffnung died prematurely at the age of thirty-four, the concerts lived on as recordings and also as performances staged in many countries. His visual art, mostly inextricable from his musical interests, is also known to many through travelling exhibitions of selected drawings as well as through numerous illustrated books.

The sheer number of his early drawings – preserved by his mother and which can therefore be seen in a continuum with the work of his professional years – makes this collection remarkable.[1] It also has particular cross-cultural significance; while his childhood was spent in an emergently fascist Germany, his adolescent years were in wartime Britain. The transfer from one country to another affected the development and eventual nature of his work in visual art.

As a caricaturist and an illustrator, Gerard Hoffnung is a different kind of artist from the others featured in this investigation, but his work was no less a response to social, cultural and artistic experience. He was born in Berlin in 1925, the only child of a middle-class German-Jewish family. His mother, very interested in the arts and remembered as a fine pianist, also drew and painted a little. She saved her son's many draw-ings without apparent discrimination even in the earliest years when there is much that others might have ignored. She meticulously dated most of the drawings, sometimes giving quarters as well as whole years and recording in German the comments her son made at the time about some of them.

It takes little imagination to understand the tensions which must have permeated family life at that time and in that place, even within a protective family circle. Gerard's first years were lived in a turbulent nation increasingly threatened by sinister political developments. His first, already prolific, infant draw-ings refer to an inner imagination, but his imagery soon began to reflect some of those outer tensions. That the playground of his first school adjoined Himmler's private garden is a poignant, symbolic fact of Gerard's early life.

There was probably great encouragement; the volume of work is considerable. Materials were obvi-ously plentiful: pencils, crayons, paint and also pens dipped in black ink, and an apparently inexhaustible supply of usable paper, in loose pages torn from sketchbooks or in some exercise and notebooks. Although they are better annotated than in other similar archives, not all the drawings can be reliably sequenced. The earliest recorded dates are at five years,

7.1 Gerard Hoffnung, *Soldier with sun and kite*, 1930 (age 5)

tinuous lines in which noses are merely protruding bumps. Shading conveys clothing or different skin colours. In these first sketches there is just a hint of quirky humour (in facial expression), a touch of aggression (in gestures) and an instinct to characterize figures, however crudely. Importantly for his future development, the techniques he learned seem to have remained fluid rather than frozen, facilitating new discoveries through their flexible use rather than inhibiting them by rigid application.

By six years, Gerard's drawings were compulsively experimental, not only with positions for viewing the human figure but with its potential as a structure for possible modification. A circus drawing shows three performers on a baseline, with an audience simulated by regularly placed shaded circles below the line. The central figure, a clown, has abnormally long legs and is posed in a giant stride. In the same drawing a clown removes his head to obtain a laugh; this drawing heralds a preoccupation with the functional or humorous distortion of the human figure, a preoccupation to be revisited throughout Gerard's childhood, adolescent and adult life.

In this year too, the subject-matter of the drawings expanded considerably with (for instance) an airship, a horse-drawn bus, attempts at observational drawing and illustrations of New Testament themes (catalogue, 8 and 11). Specific characters appear: fat or thin ladies, men with beards and top hats, jovial Indians. To convey their personalities as well as their appearances, the construction of their bodies varies, from long rectangles with triangular skirts or shaded trouser-legs, to circles resting heavily on short boxy legs.

Instead of being presented in isolation, figures became meaningfully related, as in *Knight and Cavemen*; united in contest, the figures are very different. Some figures became the basis of first compositions: a diminutive monarch is shown crossing the sea on a canopied boat with attendants, as twin figures watch from the other side of the water (a second baseline). Another composition – a mystical scene with flying half-human figures, snowmen with haloes and a skeleton bearing a sickle – has at its centre a large shaded cube on which there is machinery being operated by some kind of devil. This drawing, *The interment* (fig.7.2), is notable for its suggestion of intuitive perspective in the central forms, as well as for its visual and symbolic complexities.

The year following Gerard's seventh birthday was a major year for his development. His drawing output became even more prolific, showing greater dexterity and an intuitive understanding of expressive techniques. He found new ways to describe and structure the human figure and used them all in turn, according

but a few drawings look as if they were created at four or possibly three.

At five years of age or before, Gerard was drawing soldiers and befeathered Indians, skulls, vehicles, fish, reptiles (serpents squiggle dramatically across pages; see catalogue, 4) and suns.[2] Conventional subjects for any such child, these are unusual in the variety of construction methods as well as their expressive achievements. A soldier has a box-like body, an egg-shaped head with a neck (double lines) and arms and legs shaded between double contours; apart from this quite sophisticated construction for this age, he is also remarkable for his light-footed and cheerful gait (see fig.7.1). Other figures, four on a sheet, seem calculatingly experimental: one unites body and head in the 'tadpole' manner and three different basic forms are used for heads – a square, a triangle and an irregular potato shape. Two of the heads are shown frontally and two in profile (one with lots of teeth).

Such apparent experiments occur again, one showing the whole figure three times: frontally, in profile and supine. Profiles recur, usually drawn as con-

7.2 Gerard Hoffnung, *The interment*, 1931 (age 6)

7.3 Gerard Hoffnung, *The swimming lesson*, 1932 (age 7)

7.4 Gerard Hoffnung, *The dead come to life again* (detail), 1932 (age 7)

to different requirements: stick figures, pseudo-stencilled figures, with bodies made from circles, armless figures (in this case possibly to acknowledge the way in which people sometimes skate with their hands held behind them). Sometimes several versions were combined into one drawing as, for example, in *The swimming lesson* (fig.7.3), where each figure has a different expressive intention. There are some examples of occlusion, noting how one object conceals another, but also the idea of one actually subsumed into another, as in, for example, *The dead come to life again* (fig.7.4).

It was while Gerard was seven years of age that the first known examples appeared of his lifelong preoccupation with making drawings about music, such as a portrayal of *Double base* [sic] *organ grinder and trumpeter*. At about this time, too, he enjoyed suggesting movement, finding graphic ways to show the force of an explosion or the sensation of speed (*Phew it goes like the wind!*, fig.7.5). He discovered the kind of drawing which can show (like an X-ray image) what is contained inside something; this often took the form of skeletal figures inside a contour of a body, quite a sophisticated anatomical and visual concept for a seven-year-old. Several drawings give form to the otherwise invisible or capture the momentary.

Redesigning the human form became an even more inventive task. In a bizarre investigation of the scale-relationship of two parts of the human body, *The unusual man* (catalogue, 50), surrealistic giant legs transport a minute human figure. Relationships between persons became important too, as in his appallingly vivid study *Dentist at work* (fig.7.6), or a *Doctor's dilemma* and a biblical episode (*The temptation*, fig.7.7).

These drawings are all witty comments on situations and the ways in which people behave in them. Some are cruelly funny about the hazards of daily life. Others display a precociously sensitive awareness of human interactions, of which *The temptation* is quite the most profound, even though it is also amusing. The figures are carefully posed: the Devil walks behind Christ, taloned hand outstretched as he cajoles (two faint reddish lines indicate his speech and its direction); Christ walks with dignity in front, bearing a staff and in profile except for his head which is turned frontally to acknowledge that he hears. But his eyes are lowered (two small arcs for the lowered lids) to avoid eye-contact with the Devil and to show both temptation and detachment.

Gerard's expressive capacity in this year had developed sufficiently to enable him to convey by simple sensitive means both the symbolism and the feeling of this mythological event. In other drawings at the same time, for example *Adam and Eve* and *Reclining nude*, he

7.5 Gerard Hoffnung, *Phew, it goes like the wind!*, 1932
(age 7)

7.6 Gerard Hoffnung, *Dentist at work*, 1932 (age 7)

7.7 Gerard Hoffnung, *The temptation*, 1932 (age 7)

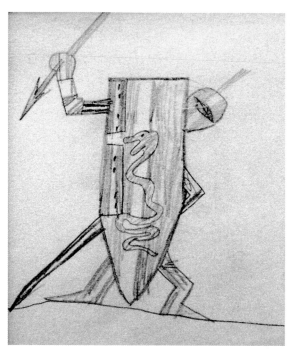

7.8 Gerard Hoffnung, *Knight behind shield*, 1933 (age 8)

7.9 Gerard Hoffnung, *Boxers*, 1933 (age 8)

is more blatantly amused with his chosen subjects. And the fine detail of *Storks at work* (pl.vɪ) reveals the high degree of his observation, control and conceptual understanding.

Around the age of eight, drawings about music, whether serious or meant to amuse, form roughly a quarter of the total number of sketches. The posture in *Knight behind shield* (fig.7.8) makes explicit the hitherto only implicit notion of figures visually blended into objects. Quite a number of mildly aggressive but usually also humorous topics emerged at this time, using effective but simple techniques to express their central ideas. The wobbling contours of the legs in *Boxers* (fig.7.9) convey the effect of a heavy punch on the chin.

Predating the real event by some three and a half decades, a witty pencil sketch (catalogue, 57) suggests the moon's apprehensive response to an imagined invasion of people from earth. *Booted figure with swastikas* is one of a few drawings that commented directly on contemporary fascism; a harsh angular drawing of a soldier and victim (fig.7.10) encapsulates what even a protected child may know about brutality; another shows the gas masks which were already being issued. The spectrum of feeling and emotion as well as information expressed at this time is extensive; there are also benevolent drawings in which children play happily and in harmony, further studies of musicians and mythological references as in *Big and little Ajax* or *Fierce dragons*.

An interplay between harsh reality, mellow observation and vigorous fantasy continued in Gerard's pen and pencil drawing throughout the two years following his ninth birthday. Until this stage, the styles of drawing were mainly his own inventions, to fit the needs of the subjects. But during this year a significant new working style appeared, with heavier contours and the typical schematic forms of the comic-book, which was to become a dominant and (some may think) undesirably tenacious influence upon his adolescent work. The archive suggests a decline in number of the drawings during the year before his tenth birthday, though they are still considerable in number and range widely across the established spectrum of themes.

The circumstances of Gerard's earliest schooling are not entirely clear; the Berlin society in which he lived as a child was eventually brought to an end by the regime, the war, death and (for some) emigration. At ten years it is known that he joined a school for 'undesirables' ('non-Aryans') which oddly was the one adjoining the Himmler household. A teacher at the school, Vera Lachman, later recorded that Gerard would 'draw caricatures on the blackboard right in the

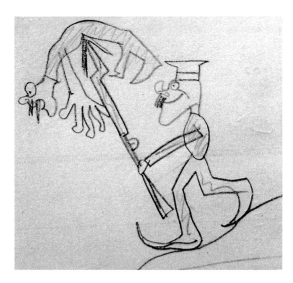

7.10 Gerard Hoffnung, *Soldier and victim*, 1933 (age 8)

midst of mechanical figures [and] turn kitchen pots into musical instruments'.[3] She added that 'at school we were aware of his unusual gifts, as an artist and a human soul, but we worried, whether he would ever be able to concentrate sufficiently on any one of his all-too-many talents. Would he become a painter, musician, a stage-performer?'[4]

Others who knew Gerard at the time have written similarly of him as an excitable, effervescent child and a rather undisciplined pupil. No one seems to remember a time when he was not engrossed in music or in drawing. He had an aptitude for quick assimilation of probably rather unorthodox performance skills, playing various instruments (including the saxophone) but without learning to read music. He loved books, especially story-books. He was frequently troublesome to his teachers and to his mother because of his incessant practical jokes, another continuing feature, as it transpired, of his entire life. He is remembered even then to have been a clever mimic and a humorous poseur, although without unkindness. The impression is of an imaginative and emotional child, possibly hyperactive, something of an entertainer, a boundary-breaker whether of rules or ideas, whose unusual skills and activities were appreciated mainly by those few adults around him who valued originality.

Between ten and eleven years of age, Gerard used a series of exercise books in which to show something of daily life in the streets of Berlin. These are more quizzical perceptions of trams and their passengers, the vehicles filled with jolly plump people; houses have cut-away windows which open to reveal figures,

7.11 Gerard Hoffnung, *One-man band*, 1936 (age 11)

7.12 Gerard Hoffnung, *The Pied Piper*, 1937 (age 12)

flowers and Jewish candelabra. The lively pencil or pen contours are filled with clear, liquid colour. In these good-natured scenarios, his drawing hovers between the comic-schematic and the more personal style which was always there somewhere at every stage of his development.

After his eleventh birthday, the volume of his drawings probably increased (or more were saved). All the earlier themes and interests are still evident. Whole orchestras vied with a quartet and a one-man band (fig.7.11) for his attention; all his musical interests found expression in numerous theatrical and orchestral studies. He illustrated fairy-tales and myths, animated inanimate objects and studied various social encounters. The style of these drawings is more whimsical and much less individual than before, with the comic-book idiom providing the principal mode of expression.

Bruno Adler, an art historian who was once a teacher at the Bauhaus and who taught Gerard during his thirteenth year, described him as 'a lively healthy boy … Inspiration lay for him in the realms of the fantastic, where magic confusion reigns and the ugly may seem comic, and the weird may be truly wonderful.'[5]

Between the ages of eleven and thirteen, a lot of extremely small drawings were made, some no more than an inch or an inch and a half in their smallest dimension. Many are in pen and wash in glowing colours, for example *The Pied Piper* (fig.7.12) or *Crocodile's head with figure*, or occasionally in gouache where the subject needed broader treatment, such as in *Portrait in blue monochrome*, an unusually powerful and sinister study. As the scale of the drawings increased in variety, so too did elements of their content; thus the

point of some of the drawings is the size-relationships within them; the crocodile holds a diminutive human between his jaws and elsewhere an entire orchestra is balanced on one trumpet (catalogue, 98).

In drawings such as *Prometheus* or *The Brandenburg Gate* the artistic conventions of the comic-book took an even stronger hold. Many also reveal a more directly illustrative intention, particularly but not only in the smaller works, such as the illustration to 'Mr Arne's Treasure', by Selmer Lagerlof (fig.7.13). Gerard at this stage was possibly more familiar with illustrations than with paintings. He had discovered how to convey mood and atmosphere, as in the impressively dramatic fire against the sky or the whimsically romantic composition *In love*. He had always known how to deal with action, but nowhere is it more darkly explicit than in the powerful illustration *Murder* (fig.7.14).

Opinion differs amongst writers as to the principal artistic influences on Gerard as he approached adolescence. It has been suggested (for instance by William Feaver in his 'Masters of Caricature') that the 'shorthand graphic conventions' and 'economical line' of the German humorist Wilhelm Busch (1832–1908) were

7.13 Gerard Hoffnung, Illustration to *Mr Arne's Treasure*,
1937 (age 12)

7.14 Gerard Hoffnung, *Murder*, 1937 (age 12)

responsible for aspects of the Hoffnung style,[6] although Bruno Adler did not agree.[7] Gerard's drawings do exhibit some of the same concerns as Busch's: for movement allied to comedy, for the relationships between people, or between people and animated objects. Something of the simplicity, even at times crudity, of form of the Busch drawings is echoed in the drawing style employed by Gerard between his tenth and fourteenth years. He would certainly have had access to Busch's work through the pages of the popular books in which Busch presented what were at the time innovatory picture-stories, presaging the modern comic-strip. However, many of these interests had originated in Gerard's drawing some years earlier, even if they were subsequently stimulated by acquaintance with Busch.

As the boy's interest in the illustration of stories grew, a simultaneous struggle seems to have been in progress (whether recognized by Gerard or not) to break from the influence of the adopted style which had taken such a grip upon his drawing. Except occasionally it remained a long-term pervasive influence, long after a recognizably consistent Hoffnung style had begun to emerge.

While the Hoffnung family were still in Germany, Gerard's mother consulted a paediatrician and two graphologists about her son's talents and future. Their verdict is contained in a predictive letter of around 1937–38 which is rather disparaging about the drawing:

He is gifted artistically but not only for drawing, which both graphologists see only as an expression of his great imagination, which is of hundred per cent importance; his drawing is only the form which his skill and gift for observation [takes] and he uses to aid his imagination until now. His absentmindedness and lack of mental discipline (altogether everything negative) is the natural consequence of such a gifted person. After all there must be some weakness somewhere that cannot be changed and partly it will improve with time when he grows reasonable.[8]

The large volume of Gerard's work from his thirteenth year marks the final period of the Hoffnung family's residence in Berlin. It is perhaps surprising – and a further demonstration of his mother's tenacity and interest if one were needed – that she managed to include so much of his work in the family luggage when hastily leaving the country. The family travelled from Berlin via St Moritz to Italy, where Gerard stayed while his parents went to Palestine (later renamed Israel) to investigate the quality of the schools in that country. These did not meet his mother's requirements for her son and she concluded that schooling in England might prove more satisfactory. Mother and son journeyed on to England, arriving there in 1939, just before the onset of war between England and Germany.

The fewer surviving drawings of his fourteenth year may have been accomplished before or after leaving Germany; it is difficult to say. In *Walking newspaper* (catalogue, 162), done at thirteen years, newspaper and man are again merged for humorous effect. There was more repetition than innovation at this time, apart from some advances in technique: a greater deftness in the use of pencil (as opposed to pen) and in the sensitive application of thin colour.

There are no drawings specifically identifiable for Gerard's fifteenth year, but by the time he attained his fifteenth birthday in 1940 he was certainly in England, learning English and settled with his mother in the Hampstead district of London. He soon began to record some of the phenomena of war as it affected his new country; like the English sculptor Henry Moore, he found the soft, rounded forms of people sleeping on the platforms of underground railway stations during air raids to be a fascinating subject (see *Underground shelter*). But in that there seems to have been little change in style since he had created *The Brandenburg Gate* some three years before. However a visual comment on Hitler (*Adolf the Decorator*) is much in keeping with propaganda caricature of that time, contemptuous and defiant. *Toboggan with running legs* is a further, this time gleefully funny, repetition of the reorganized-body theme.

It is interesting that the humour of these drawings is more benevolent and less harsh than in those from the early Berlin years, in keeping, one may suppose, with the different social and political environment of the time in Britain. That the drawings seem to reflect this difference of feeling does not imply that either the child or the adolescent was conscious of it. Nor does it mean that the horrific ceased to be of interest, but rather that fear was displaced by fun, so that eventually, as a family friend has written, 'the chuckle … ousted the shiver'.[9]

Gerard's awareness of drawing techniques was growing, however. His drawing style soon changed, even though elements of previous techniques continued to exist within the new. He began to use light and shade, not just to cast shadows as in earlier drawing, but also to articulate form and make it exciting. This was linked to his discovery of the richness of cross-hatching in ink and thereby the possibility of creating infinite tonal depth. Earlier and patently successful but stereotyped methods were no longer enough for the more realistic, more imaginative and more fantastic ideas that he now wanted to express.

Nearly all the known drawings at the age of sixteen were created at a London independent school, Highgate, where the curriculum was of the most formal and attitudes to somewhat unusual pupils probably inflexible. There were no art lessons as such; most of Gerard's drawings were produced during the German lessons. By this diversionary strategy, the German master solved the problem of a pupil who was in no need of his teaching; he asked him to illustrate German folk-tales. Pens and watercolours were provided; the resultant colour sketches are vivid, as though the use of such colour was a heady experience. Seemingly, Gerard used the opportunity and the materials to do other drawings which had nothing to do with the subjects set, expressing humorous incidents with inventive vigour. The composition *Fly-hunt* (catalogue, 189) depicts a room seen from a height well above the heads of the figures in it; the action is graphically enhanced by this elevated viewing position.

Gerard was obviously at home with his own subject-matter. But most of the drawings based on illustrating the prescribed subjects seem more constrained and unrepresentative of either his sensitive eye or his dexterity with pen and wash; they are also reversions to old, rather Germanic images, in keeping of course with the origins of the stories as well as the history of the young artist.

More typical of his skills and his gentle anarchy are the illicitly created drawings which caricature the masters of the school (catalogue, 173–79). Reminiscent of the four experimental heads which Gerard had done at five years, these heads also explore geometric variations; the resultant portraits are, however, finely and economically drawn, the humour is essentially genial and the likenesses possibly strong. On the backs too of some of the other 'commissioned' drawings are minute and intriguing visual pencilled 'thoughts': a fly, a small detailed biplane, a smoking pipe (anticipating one which the adult Hoffnung eventually owned). In these spontaneous sketches, the style emerges as independent, sensitive and personal, no longer needing the support of any adopted conventions, though sometimes choosing to utilize them.

While he was sixteen, Gerard successfully submitted some small drawings to *Lilliput* magazine, a publication small in format but large in popularity in Britain during the 1940s and early 1950s. Though amusing, these drawings are relatively poor achievements compared with the illustrations and caricatures of the same year. Indeed, by his seventeenth birthday he was showing a professional confidence even though he had not up till then received any professional tuition. He was now drawing almost entirely in pen and ink, having developed with experience a deeper awareness of the qualities of line, mass and rich texture which pen could express.

7.15 Gerard Hoffnung, *Gee up, my fine horses*, 1942 (age 17)

By now envisaging a career as an illustrator, he began designing his illustrations with more obvious aesthetic intention beyond the essential demands of the narrative, as in *Gee up my fine horses* (fig.7.15). This new aesthetic awareness is highlighted in a study done at seventeen of a sleeping head (catalogue, 208), in which the quality of the drawing is obviously paramount over the subject.

An excellent cartoon done at seventeen years, *The operation* (fig.7.16), brings together many of the themes and accomplishments prevalent so far: humour, the interest in music, the preoccupation with the relative sizes of objects, caricature and the explicit meaning conveyed by the grouping of characters.

Gerard first played with pen and ink at around seven years when he created *Storks at work* (catalogue, 40; pl.VI) and by the age of nine he could manipulate the medium vigorously and well, as in *Three musicians* (catalogue, 82). The pen as a medium may have been a key factor in his further development. He remained more dependent on the styles of others while he clung

7.16 Gerard Hoffnung, *The operation*, 1942 (age 17)

7.17 Gerard Hoffnung, *A cadenza*

to pencil or used pen in the same way as pencil to delineate outlines of form which were to be filled in with colour wash. But a natural personal drawing system emerged as he found that with his pen he could draw into the form rather than around it, providing tonal and textural richness. The mass of drawings which he undertook at seventeen, such as 205 in the catalogue, and at eighteen (catalogue, 213), before he arrived at art school, seem collectively to celebrate this new independence from earlier adopted styles, even though those had paved the path of his development.

Hoffnung, as a mature artist, continued to express many of the themes which had interested him in childhood. He constantly reinvented the human form (see *A staccato*; *A legato*; *A crescendo*; *A pizzicato*; *A cadenza*, fig.7.17 and *A drum-roll*),[10] blended it visually into other objects as in *Jazz*[11] and compared its character similarities to some of them (*Man with an anglepoise lamp*).[12] Relationships between people as well as their roles in life remained a life-long interest, whether they were fellow-travellers, members of an orchestra or two people having a row.[13]

The pen, which he had first used at seven years but never fully exploited until the age of fifteen, became the most important medium for Hoffnung in adult life. If seen in the original, his mature drawings show that it came to be used with exceptional delicacy and great innovation for expressive ends as, for example, in *The vibraphone*.[14]

Traces of the influence of the comic-book always remained in his work, as in the grotesque heads and feet of his cartoon *The trout quintet*.[15] But ultimately his style owes much to an even earlier time, to the uniquely personal forms of his earliest infant sketching, as though returning to some essence of the personality of the artist which remained constant throughout. It is this constancy of ideas, techniques, vision and especially spirit over the thirty-four years of Gerard's life which makes the whole collection of drawings so remarkable.

8

A professional journey:
Sarah Raphael (1960–)

When I was a child I never questioned what I was doing, I just painted with enthusiasm and the memory of that tided me over when I was [later] painting with confusion and fear

Sarah Raphael, in an interview, 1991

By the early 1990s, and in her early thirties, the English artist Sarah Raphael had succeeded in establishing a place among contemporary British artists working in London. A major show of her work attracted acclaim, patrons, purchasers and new commissions. Following attention from the media and critics she was among those nominated in 1992 for the prestigious, if controversial, (British) Turner Prize. Had her work been more directly avant-garde, she might well have been one of the finalists but in that arena it would have seemed too traditional, with landscape and portraiture as subject-matter, and mostly oils, gouache and acrylic as media.

It was and is nonetheless challenging, individual and increasingly powerful. Visitors to her 1992 London exhibition might have perceived an Italian influence from the work of early Renaissance painters such as Piero della Francesca and Uccello,[1] unsurprising for an artist who had seen a great deal in Italian museums as a young child. The darker intensity of some of her work was also associated with German Romanticism and some contemporary Polish art which similarly expresses a 'silent anguish' for the suffering and predicament of the Jews.[2] But there are links with English art too, perhaps with the figurative mysticism, though without the religion, of Stanley Spencer.

The circumstances of Sarah Raphael's childhood and adolescence have some unusual aspects. Both the history of her family and the familial and social environment in which she was nurtured can be argued as being formative in her emergence as an artist. But her progression was erratic and the 'journey' less than smooth at times.

Her father, Frederic Raphael, came as a child from the United States to live in England, just prior to the outbreak of war in Europe in 1939. Old schoolbooks exist which show that by the age of nine he was already an accomplished writer, who could construct imaginative stories of considerable sophistication. Settling in to life in his new country may have been an uneasy experience, but he successfully negotiated the English educational system, eventually taking a Cambridge degree. His years as a student there and afterwards were soon the subject of two very successful novels which made him widely known and strengthened an already flourishing career as author and critic.

A consequence of this success was that the family travelled widely. Sarah was born in East Bergholt in Suffolk, the middle child of three, with an older brother, Paul, and a younger one, Stephen. She was from the beginning an equable infant who rarely cried, content to lie for long periods watching others. Her first major journey was at five months to Spain, where the family stayed until she was thirteen months old. This was the first of a series of residential periods in different countries which typified family life during her early years and probably affected Sarah's later interests. From the age of two, and beginning in Rome, she deeply enjoyed accompanying her parents to museums. When not living elsewhere, home was initially in Suffolk; later a new and permanent home was established in Essex.

Wherever home was temporarily located, art played an important part in daily life. It was in the first place something her father did for a living and which caused him to be shut away for periods each day. She soon understood the discipline of the artist even though the work itself, literary in his case and emerging from a typewriter, was not necessarily visible at the time. As very young children, Paul and Sarah would play on the terrace near Frederic without interrupting him. But she and her brothers were nonetheless made to feel participants in what he did, travelling as a family wherever his work took him and sharing in its developments and difficulties, even going on the set when a film scripted by their father was being made.

By example, Frederic gave his daughter an invaluable and vital understanding of the nature of being an artist, that it was not a state of mind so much as a relentless and unceasing occupation. Fulfilling this criterion obsessively throughout childhood, she knew she was already an artist rather than trying to become one. When her confidence later fluctuated, it was not in the family environment but when peers and teachers challenged her.

Older members of the family, notably her father's mother and her mother's sister, produced art of the visual kind, the latter having some strong facility as a painter. Paul (her elder by two and a half years) was also keen on drawing as a small boy, but was soon discouraged by his sister's rapidly advancing skills. Her mother, Sylvia, drew a lot as a child although she remembers no painting, but she wrote stories as a teenager and has a strong literary interest. From the beginning, Sylvia was fascinated by all the children's drawings. Quietly encouraging them all, she began to save and store what they drew. The collection was rapidly dominated by Sarah's more prolific material, even though much may have been discarded by Sarah herself.

After the family moved into their Essex home, it was decided to acquire a trained nanny to care for the children and, by chance, the one chosen proved to be quite artistic. At a key moment in the infant Sarah's intellectual as well as tactile development, the nanny instigated inventive and creative games involving an enormous sand tray and much finger-painting. Sarah responded ecstatically to this; her mother recalls that the two-year-old seemed astonishingly more capable than many children twice her age, having a strong imagination and an unusually long attention span. She was a child who was quite content to be on her own, playing for hours on the floor with the diminutive contents of boxes. She quickly learned to talk, having been able to sing in tune even before that. Although Paul was older and of course physically that much stronger (and has always shown acute visual awareness), Sarah rapidly overtook him in many skills. Although his work was 'more wonderful' than hers, she feels he lacked the obsession which fuelled her own approach.

As with so many small children, Sarah's first ventures into drawing were about animals, particularly horses which she was 'mad about'. At four she had already seen (and still remembers) the lion sculptures on the Gate at Mycenae in Greece; she studied them intently and recreated them on a hotel note pad. The earliest saved examples of her drawings are probably those in which linked circular forms represent body, legs (two), head, ears (two), tail and often testicles; they have near-human faces. In subsequent drawings she adopted a different strategy, creating the entire form in one continuous heavy line, which resulted in a crude but often surprisingly powerful image, lending itself eventually to a hint of stance and body movement beyond the initial diagrammatic effect.

Possibly these two methods existed in parallel for a while, since the former drawings developed an anthropomorphic sophistication, being reinterpreted into crying elephants, for example; the latter were embroidered with additions, notably saddles and (stick-figure) riders. In due course they were combined in one image, the horse still in continuous angular line and the rider in separate rounder parts. The representations varied daily, being sometimes gleefully expressive and at others rigidly less exciting. One or two of these early horse drawings emphasize the tail or a curious upright mane, the beginning of a passion for hair in all its textures and forms. At around four years, the characteristically longer horse head appeared.

First representations focusing on humans are well-defined. Given that most children at this stage (perhaps four years) undersize the body in relation to the head, it is nevertheless obvious in these drawings that heads, especially hirsute ones, were of paramount interest to Sarah, whether drawn gesturally or with a regular edge. These, too, are not just figures but characters: though simple, they have expressions; their heads are turned or the pupils in their eyes swivel to confront the viewer; hair is richly shaded with a thick pencil or felt pen; clothing is often more loosely shaded to suggest heavy and sometimes almost tartan patterning. Some figures have visible mechanical or electronic interiors, an idea the 'X-ray' implications of which have fascinated innumerable children.

At four, Sarah was attending a Montessori school where children were especially encouraged to make patterns; at home she drew small action compositions with figures or vehicles. A chalk sketch on black paper of figures of varying sizes was drawn by linking balloon shapes (fig.8.1), an eloquently simple visual conception of a family. This theme is recurrent, no doubt initially an expression of personal situation but soon prompted by observations in other countries of different families, especially poor ones which she saw at the time as 'in tiny little homes and having to muck in together'.

Some of these drawings are in pencil but the preferred medium was felt-tip pen, offering a depth of colour and richness of line and mass unequalled by

8.1 Sarah Raphael, *Family*, c.1964 (age 4)

any other available medium. Sarah was very perceptive; some time after her fifth birthday and when she was attending St Paul's Girls School in London, the pattern of extended hymn books at morning assembly caught her eye, spawning a number of drawings which exploit repetitions. When she was not observing the world directly, inspiration came from her books, from *Babar the Elephant*, or *James and the Giant Peach*.

School and home were not easily compatible for Sarah. Reflecting on her difficulties at the time, her mother Sylvia describes 'a deliberate family policy' which valued individuality above conformity. Consequently Sarah may have seemed undisciplined, not revealing at school the more conventional academic skills, nor her true worth as an independent mind. Except for one perceptive teacher who was able to stimulate and encourage her drawing, she was viewed unsympathetically and recalls that she thought of home as a refuge, and of school as threatening; the latter frustrated her, cramped her style and 'she got smaller', Sylvia remembers.

It would be difficult to put a date on her first intentional portrayals of humour. There is a kind of cuteness, linked with fashion detail (such as high heels) in some of the drawings of this period; some narrative drawings show people no longer statically contemplating the viewer but actively involved in events. Details of clothing and physique are of less

consequence; figures are even diagrammatically distorted to show their physical attitudes or intentions. In a drawing about Christmas shopping, the body of the flying angel is curved (in a manner reminiscent of Chagall's similar figures) to accentuate the notion of flight. In a later illustration (to Roald Dahl's *James and the Giant Peach*), the simplistic figures have constructed ladders and are seen climbing into the clouds to make hailstones. This is not in itself funny but it reveals the beginnings of an economical manipulation of form and circumstance which could become so. In a portrayal of a carriage drawn by a winged horse, and in other similar works of this period and idiom, where there is an attempt at indicating distance through figure sizes, there is a joyous comedic element in the cherubs flying alongside (see fig.8.2). But when comedy in due course became the main intention, it was usually supported by balloon speech or other verbal inscriptions.

The identification by children with their images at the time of creating them is easy to observe. Sarah's drawings at five and six years became complex renderings of remembered or imagined scenes, often about children of her own age playing together – taunting, assaulting or racing round each other – or about horse races where the jockeys or spectators have something to shout. In the latter drawings, with the races proceeding across the page from left to right, horses and riders are sometimes drawn half on and half off the paper, about which she points out that having mentally entered the imagined place, 'that world continued outside the picture-frame and was very real to me' (fig.8.3).[3]

While many of the figure studies are panoramic, with active figures, singly or in groups, fairly evenly scattered across the paper, some feature a central cluster of figures that are large on the sheet as though for Sarah to deal more with their personalities and relationships than with their actions. During her time at St Paul's and for a while after, a number of black felt-pen outline sketches which are more explicitly humorous were accomplished in this way. Happiness and a cheeky exuberance are evident; accompanying writing, as a sort of diary, sometimes indicates that they are about Sarah, her brothers and her friends.

By the time Sarah was seven years of age, she had already spent time in Rome, Spain and Greece before the family were temporarily resident in South America. Wherever she went, she would pack her trunks with drawing paper and, if there was schooling, she would insist that the teachers gave her time to draw. But it was her regular holiday visits to the Greek island of Ios which gave her the most enduring delight and where, according to her mother, she has always been 'more herself ... than anywhere'. With Paul she hunted

8.2 Sarah Raphael, *Coach and winged children*, 1964 (age 4)

8.3 Sarah Raphael, *Horse race*, 1965–66 (age 5–6)

8.4 Sarah Raphael, *That place – Ios*, c.1994, oils,
121.92 × 153.67 cm

insects, made homes in caves, rode donkeys and drew pictures in the sand, living out their adventurous fantasies. Her childhood experience of the island has haunted her imagination ever since and is immortalized in an oil painting twenty years on, *That place – Ios* (fig.8.4).

Around the age of seven, she began 'to take the trouble [as she now expresses it] to make the colour of the faces as opposed to drawing them' and to attach importance to the colouring of figures and clothing, with all the visual consequences of that for the enrichment of each drawing. She was greatly inspired in this by a fascination with the exotically uniformed military bands so prevalent around her during the South American interlude. But it also stemmed from her earlier acquaintance with the images of the *Beano* and

similar children's comic papers. Of one drawing of this period, which shows each of the members of an entire football team as a linear display, she remembers that she wanted to show how she would draw the characters as compared with the style used in the *Beano*. Hers are more finely differentiated and the clothing is more subtly coloured; they otherwise owe much to the style of that journal, big-eyed and bumpy-kneed. This is a drawing which, with name labels and other details (such as spotted shorts), mocks her imagined subjects rather than sharing the joke with them.

Between seven and nine, Sarah's drawings developed a number of parallel themes. Earlier diary-like drawings with writing were superseded by illustrated stories, many of which were made to entertain Stephen. A story about 'Tomy [sic] Bee', dedicated on its title

8.5 Sarah Raphael, *Dispute*, c.1967 (age 7)

8.6 Sarah Raphael, *Urban scene*, c.1967–68 (age 7–8)

page to Stephen and Paul, depicts in fairly simple forms the birth, christening ceremony and subsequent family feast of the central character; however, each of the figures along one side of the table has a different posture, making the drawing more intriguing, less trivial. With increasing sophistication and as the stories became more involved, the pictures reclaimed importance over the text, which became an ingredient of the images themselves, locked into capacious speech-bubbles.

Another form of story-telling, not dependent upon the turning of pages but upon sequential images on the same page, was arising as a key activity out of her comic-book experiences. In one of the earliest of these, the sequences are separated from each other by organic rather than geometric lines, which lends to the vigorous movements of the characters an additional dynamism; the figures themselves are gesturally outlined but the economy of the actions by which they were created is their strength; with successive sequenced stories, the pictures are more geometrically

boxed and the figures more formally outlined and coloured but also more calculatingly poised (see, for example, fig.8.5).

Thirdly, there were times when Sarah worked on drawings with a brother or her father, either on the same sheet of paper or on two sheets later combined. At the time she had clear feelings about the validity of such pieces; while the shared experience was greatly enjoyed, she 'wouldn't have shown the picture to anyone because it wasn't all mine'. Conversely what was entirely hers was very important; when she was about six, her teacher at school had taken one of Sarah's drawings for herself, without permission from the resentful artist.

There are other seemingly more separate experimental drawings, in some of which Sarah shows her awareness of their contexts in the mainstream of art. Of one monochrome image, possibly done with a brush, she surmises that 'I would have seen something rather grown-up, a landscape – it's self-consciously arty' (fig.8.6). And she was beginning to be aware of herself as female and sexual; a coloured sketch made at around seven or eight years shows her invention of a 'beauty machine' which could perhaps do wonders for those who felt the need; there is also a gradually increasing incidence of drawings of fascinating ginger-bearded and impressively hairy-chested males.

The activity of drawing was not undertaken solely in two dimensions. Her facility for the three-dimensional, which had been evident so soon, may have been sustained by various family friends who were sculptors: in the early years by Charlotte Gordon, and later in her adolescence by Michael Ayrton, although Ayrton's ideas are remembered by Sarah as more influential upon her than his work. As well as models made of paper, there was also spirited clay-modelling of animals and humans. One may question why Sarah did not eventually emerge as an artist working in three dimensions, given her at least equal flair for sculpture. The seductive tactile power of surface texture, of curving planes and of weighted forms in space is, however, as much the playground of the painter, by inference, as of the sculptor in actuality, and more apparently so in the work of specific painters. While she does no three-dimensional work professionally now, her paintings and portraits are continuingly concerned with these phenomena.

Given her early sculptural fluency, Sarah's two-dimensional work did not so soon reflect an awareness of three dimensions and an intuitive expression of objects in perspective as one might have expected; it was longer still before she began to apply this to human forms, which otherwise remained fairly flat, the actions increasingly important but shown quite diagrammatically. Clothing patterns, hair and, above all, personality were the most important features of most of her drawings between the ages of seven and eleven. But at one primary school there was a good opportunity to work in clay in three dimensions and from the outset this had great appeal, a revisiting of her earliest flair for modelling and model-making. Around the age of nine she made family groups, single figures such as *Seated clay figure* (fig.8.7), a kissing couple reminiscent of Rodin's and simple relief studies of horses and riders.

By this time, Paul had been boarding at Bedales School in Hampshire for two years and Sarah was desperate to follow him there, although he was not enjoying it. Perhaps she was merely competing with him by following in his footsteps, or she had glimpsed something about the school's art department that looked enticing, or maybe, as Sylvia affectionately proposes, she envied the gifts that Paul received on his weekend visits home. Although any good local school would have been her mother's choice, Sylvia was happy for her to go there, since art was certainly strong in the curriculum.[4]

In the event, Sarah was ecstatic for her first term at Bedales and then experienced a period of homesickness before settling down to the rhythm of boarding-school life and the possibilities of the art department. There she found a teacher who was wise enough to recognize her potential and to know how best to help her; he encouraged her but left her alone as much as possible, with space to develop. This for Sarah was a great relief from earlier interference at primary schools and she says, 'I just wanted to paint; I was not overly encouraged in the Science Department!'

In the development of drawing fluency, eleven

8.7 Sarah Raphael, *Seated clay figure*, 1969 (age 9)

seems to be a key age at which an escalation of knowledge, skill and confidence projects many committed children into a new and exciting near-adolescent phase, while for others the impetus begins to fall away. So this is a good moment to ask whether Sarah's earliest work before that age gave any clear indication of an eminent professional future. Except for her first infant achievements, which clearly caught her mother's attention at the time and impressed with their flair and unusual competence, much of her childhood work after that and for several years is conventional, structurally uninventive and sometimes fairly crude. It lacks obvious precocity such as is shown by some exceptional children in the form of sharp observations, deft manipulative skills, competent translations from three dimensions into two and speedy adoption of cultural conventions for drawing.

But her strengths were not in that form. She was more interested in human interaction – caricature,

8.8 Sarah Raphael, *School photograph*, c.1969–70 (age 9–10)

8.9 Sarah Raphael, *Prisoner reading*, c.1970–71 (age 10–11)

galloping or speed, throwing, kicking, dancing, talking and all the other intriguing manifestations of an unstable but intoxicating and largely social world – than in nature and architecture or form for form's sake. This attitude and these phenomena might have signalled her future: the way in which one or other of her drawings captured an attitude, an expression, a style, a character or an event, with a graphic touch which makes the drawing come alive.

The characterizations are especially rich in Sarah's drawings and paintings about posed school groups. At Bedales she was made especially aware of the process of growing up through the formality of the year-by-year classes and the ranking from smallest to tallest in the annual photograph. The characters were, however, her own inventions; she was engrossed 'in making up who they were and what they were like' (see *School photograph*, fig.8.8), different from many of the multi-figured balloon-speech drawings in which her preoccupation was with what the figures were doing.

Around this time her father gave her a box of oils; her first attempt at working in the medium shows that it caused an increase in scale; otherwise she initially held to the same technique of dark outlines and colour infilling, although at least one portrait head has more solidity than those before it. By her second year at her new school, she was working there in oils too as well as in gouache, with some guided experiments in

8.10 Sarah Raphael, *Runners*, c.1971 (age 11)

monochrome gouache. Like other children of this age, she was moving towards a new feeling for objects as existing in space. Gradually more aware of the visual consequences of light and the way in which forms in the same space are linked and can be orchestrated by light, she painted a prisoner reading in his cell; the painting depends for its effect upon the lightbulb over his head and the way in which his open book and the rough cell walls are illuminated (fig.8.9).

Her work was moving now, albeit erratically, towards the illustration of the ideas of others as well as her own, although sometimes these were in an analytical or cataloguing rather than a story-recounting mode; after reading *Jane Eyre* at school, she laid out in lines on a page a series of full-length portraits of every character in the book. Contemporary pop-stars received much the same treatment, although they might be shown less statically, singing into microphones or addressing each other across the page with fervour and

wit. There is a lot of drawing-as-game here, the enactment of real or fantasy situations with actual or imagined individuals.

A significant painting at this time, hung in a show of children's paintings at the City Gallery in Southampton, shows sprinters in a race, seen as though from above and with the composition constructed through the strong, white vertically placed markings of the race-track under and behind the figures and through the oblique angle of the figure shadows (fig.8.10). Paintings made some twenty years later (now in private collections) show similar running figures (for example, *Boys chasing a squirrel IV*), observe them from a similar angle (*Whilst Attempting to Escape*) or have the same vertically banded composition (*The villager II*).

The paintings and drawings based on ideas initiated by teachers in the school art-room were, at least in Sarah's early adolescence, fairly ordinary, a product of

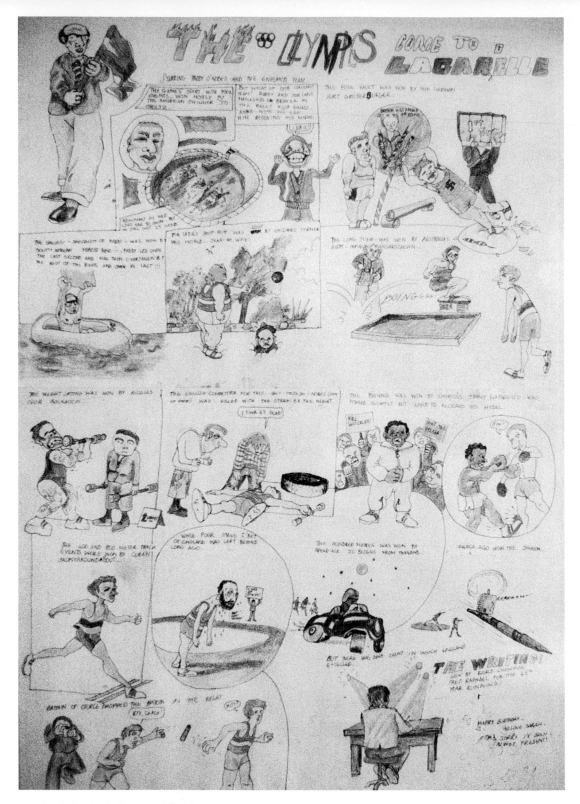

8.11 Sarah Raphael, *The Lagardelle Olympics*, c.1972 (age 12)

8.12 Sarah Raphael, *Balletic figures*, c.1972–73 (age 12–13)

tacit resignation to the initial situation rather than of actual enthusiasm. In the background much of her home-based drawing was imaginatively vigorous, wittier and often anarchic; hirsute, strong men and randy-looking lads brimming with cheeky excitability were much more inspiring as subject-matter. At school there were opportunities to draw from life and from nature, to compare the distant with the detailed, and to engage in the kind of literary and increasingly romantic illustrations at which she was becoming adroit. Unsurprisingly in view of her parents' interests, literature was a frequent source of ideas; with hind-sight Sarah feels that she could easily have become a writer herself if the pull of the visual had not been so strong. It is a significant story in this respect that when she was eight, frustrated by an order not to touch her father's typewriter, she made herself a model one of her own from paper.

Sarah's exploration of the oil medium was sustained at Bedales from early adolescence but with different influences. She remembers, when she was twelve, looking at illustrated books on art, as her painting ably

imitating Botticelli's *Venus* indicates. She was also much affected by the activities of her peers in school, by a boy who was technically very gifted and a girl, now a successful sculptor. She was still drawing on occasion for her father; a sophisticated page of sequential comic drawings, *The Lagardelle Olympics* (fig.8.11), now quite finely delineated and deftly watercoloured, compares all the Olympic winners of the various events with 'the winner of the writings' event, her father, shown as he was so frequently portrayed by Sarah, seated and facing away from the viewer towards his desk.

In these years there is an eclecticism of styles, newly virtuoso, fluent and adaptive, but showing at this point a distinct move beyond 'normal' development in this area. As the artist puts it, she 'went through a lot of styles; I did so much that didn't work' and notes the occasional piece that did, a sand-dune landscape for example, richly coloured and authoritatively com-posed, and a study of balletic figures, which was ex-hibited publicly and earned the approval of others as well as her own (fig.8.12). Her intuitive search at this

8.13 Sarah Raphael, *Portrait of Stephen*, c.1974 (age 14)

stage was for a personal style to be found through the experimental adoption of many.

Sarah is generally critical of what she accomplished in the years at Bedales. Her first interest in art books was short-lived, perhaps overwhelmed by an eager adolescent's embracing of the exuberant pop-culture all around her. For a time, 'my interest in painting was no more than dutiful', she recalls. She was anyway not really thinking about painting as 'art'; that came later. It was simply the most accessible and direct means of expression for her heady and dramatic ideas, whether about humans or about gods, goddesses and catastrophically momentous imaginings.

She now sees the work of this time as slapdash, poorly considered and inadequately resolved; all that mattered to her was 'to get the story down'. This is a reasonable appraisal from a later professional who has come to know the rigour of art. But another eye can relish the vivacity of these paintings; whatever their importance at the time or their weaknesses now, they graphically express her passionate and volatile attitude to life, people and the fervour of her own imagination. In doing so they begin to indicate the future.

The subject-matter of these works was as diverse as the styles. When she was about thirteen, Sarah was affected by reading the poetry of Siegfried Sassoon and by the film of *All Quiet on the Western Front*. She made a number of muted paintings which explored the theme of the war, including an apocalyptic battle scene in monochrome, the desolation illuminated by an exploding shell overhead; another colour sketch in close-up of wounded soldiers is a harshly compassionate image. At around fourteen, she made portraits of imaginary people and a delicate study from life of Stephen (fig.8.13), with a growing sensitivity to both form and medium. To sophisticate her own self-image,

she made a composition of several vivacious young nude females, a striking assertion of female sexuality. Another joyous painting celebrates the delights of swimming in the sea in a group, all dashing brush-strokes, fresh colour and exuberance (*Swimming in the sea*).

Many of her self-initiated drawings and paintings of the time are witty, cynical or flamboyant while the schoolwork tends to be more cautiously investigative. In the former group are innumerable pencil sketches of adolescents in satirical discussion or family members seen together; in the latter there are some well-observed colour studies of the school's grounds. One of the best paintings of this period combines techniques learned at school with a more personal interest in character and mood; a boy strolls disconsolately along the edge of a wheat field, his figure dark against the richness of the ripened crop and light sky (fig.8.14). This introspection is paralleled in a self-portrait of the same period, finely observed and drawn, and revealing a new inner serenity. Michael Ayrton's advice had been that whenever she was short of a subject, she could use herself.

In the mid-adolescent stage of schooling, prior to major examinations, the pressure is on to strengthen art students' observation and recording skills, with a plethora of studies of natural forms, artefacts and drawings from life. In the long term this process sometimes damages expressive fluency. Sarah responded to these demands with a display of versatility in drawing anything from a soft bag to a piece of complex, unyielding machinery (fig.8.15). Judging by her other work at the time, she already knew these tasks to be no more important in themselves than muscle-training is to a dancer, experiences to be gone through as instrumental to the long-term aim of developing personal expressive skills. She was, in any case, at a school where this was understood by some teachers.

She nevertheless found it difficult to respond to their call for a more open method of working; 'They wanted me to be free and uninhibited but I didn't want it that way.' Particularly in portraiture she was already into a deep and enduring quest for the personality of a subject, which she could only find through intense perception and analysis, greatly in contrast with her earlier caricatures, where character emerged so speedily from gesture guided by feeling. While a more open approach to the use of different media at this time might have been creatively productive, it is true that her instinctive choice of approach laid the groundwork for the portraits of ten or fifteen years later, often small and full of the kind of 'information' which seems to present, through its very intensity, the aura of a person beyond mere likeness.

8.14 Sarah Raphael, *Figure in cornfield*, 1973–74 (age 13–14)

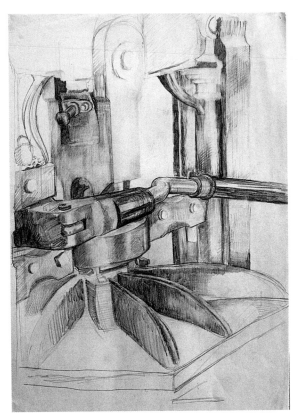

8.15 Sarah Raphael, *Still life*, c.1975–76 (age 15–16)

Before leaving Bedales, Sarah had to prepare a portfolio to take to an interview for a place at Camberwell College of Art. She was not quite sixteen when some of those drawings were made. They included sketches resembling studies from life (such as fig.8.16) but which are in fact imaginary figures, in soft but rich pencil and entirely plausible as characters.

The transition from school to college was uneasy. From studying in a place where her exceptional skills were recognized and where she was given considerable autonomy, she now felt more like other students and was being tightly directed. The process was painful and she hated it, although she recognized her need of it. Fortunately Frederic and Sylvia's support had prepared her for this; impressing upon her their view of her exceptional talent, they had also given her to understand that she would achieve little of consequence without commitment and effort; 'I was shown that I must hold my love of what I did sacred.'

Initially tuition at Camberwell was more positive than sensitive, although a tutor's role in this inductive stage is to shake loose a student's preconceptions, in preparation for new discoveries. Sarah later wondered if some of the tutors were really good enough to nurture the passion for painting that many students revealed. To progress within the system, one had to embrace the Camberwell philosophy, denying their individual beliefs. 'I did for a while; I lost my trust in my own judgment', Sarah recalls. As an antidote to this, she invested a lot of time in visits to galleries.

At Camberwell in the mid-1970s, unlike at many other British art schools, the life class remained important and Sarah had prepared for this with evening classes near her school. Her first life drawings at Camberwell, however, reflect the unease of a new student in a prestigious institution; they show a lack of confidence and even sometimes of the knowledge of anatomy and form that was shown earlier. But change came quickly; the conventions of Camberwell were soon assimilated; she discovered the sensual dynamism of the nude and how to deploy nuances of light and shadow and the medium to capture them. The best of the Camberwell life drawings are strongly professional in her facility with different media and her exploitation of style. The heads of the models received special attention, with their features often engrossingly explored to a greater depth than in other parts of a drawing.

Sarah at Camberwell became confused by the notion of abstraction and how she should deal with it. Some attempts to edge towards it are recorded in some watercolours, probably from imagination, and one from a window in the family home at Lagardelle, where colour seems only tentatively associated with form. A pencil drawing shows by its angularities that she was finding a temporary haven in the work of Cézanne, that initiating explorer of abstraction and of the 'structure of nature'.[5] Sketches in watercolours of Dordogne landscapes suggest that Cézanne was close to her mind on location too (see *Coastal landscape*, fig.8.17). A composite painting, done away from art school (fig.8.18), shows her obsession with him more directly, through the books portrayed in the foreground. Two interior studies, one simply executed and mainly in soft washes and the other richly in oils, thoughtfully structure the composition in straight lines, angles, hard and soft edges allied to curving, fluctuating contours and variations of tone.

In her final year Sarah nearly succumbed to professional and emotional tensions and to falling out of studentship altogether, but she was supported at a critical moment by two tutors who understood the nature of her problems. Their teaching styles were very different. One involved her in a series of life-size still-life paintings, which bolstered her confidence at that particular time. Another's teaching strategy was to

8.16 Sarah Raphael, *Study of a boy*, 1977 (age 17)

8.17 Sarah Raphael, *Coastal landscape*, 1978 (age 18)

challenge her ideas ruthlessly, which, paradoxically, she found highly constructive, as he had no doubt intended.

Art colleges usually make their students conscious of contemporary innovations and movements as well as of tradition. Most students arrive at art college with a strong fluency of technique and a passion for a particular art form which they hope to develop. The best students are usually those who absorb a broader view of art while blazing through it a personal trail of their own, reacting greedily to some of the proffered ideas but also fervently rejecting others.

Already at Bedales, and later with even greater difficulty at Camberwell, Sarah seems to have experienced a problem that is formidable for many artists as students: how to relate a powerful expressive intention to a passion for the evidence of the visible. In Sarah's later years, that problem has found its resolution in works which variously explore that relationship. The fine portraits and dark landscapes of her twenties and early thirties have as much to do with surface – marks and forms in abstraction – as with literal images.

Ultimately, as William Boyd suggests, she has found her own position as an artist by 'blending the real strengths and resources of [her] gifts as a draftsman and painter with the resources of … twentieth-century art'.[6]

That appraisal seems to be epitomised by her 1998 exhibition, called 'Strip', in London, with its allusions to 1960s Pop Art (pl.VII). Some critics found these new works unrelated to anything she had shown before and thought that she had reinvented herself as a painter yet again. They had missed her earlier fascination with surface, its textures and illusions, developed in the *Desert* series three years before and gloriously exploited in *Strip 8* and *Strip 9*.

But there is a longer perspective for these new works. In 1997, after a serious illness, she found herself sketching in a format recognizably that of the comic-paper sequential boxed storylines she had used so much as an adolescent. This cell/grid format initiated the *Strip* paintings and determined the final canvases, even when (in the later ones) the black contours have gone and their presence is only tacit to the compo-

8.18 Sarah Raphael, *Still life with portraits*, c.1977 (age 17)

sitions and the comic-paper idioms they involve. These paintings are not a new beginning but are eloquently autobiographical, a dramatically explicit link between past and present which reveals the long 'journey' she has undertaken.

That journey was not objectively predetermined. For Sarah Raphael, doing has always been the thing, with art that is direct and practical rather than arising from detached contemplation. She has consistently upheld the view, even before she gave form to it, that 'I don't like the idea of decision-making on a cold intellectual level. I believe those ideas should come from the process of painting.'

9

Displacing the demon:
David Downes (1971–)

I gained solace in my own world, and began to express my obscure thoughts … The drawings were of things around me I wished to change.

David Downes, 1993

David Downes has become an artist: that simple statement masks a more than usually complex achievement. After a long period of professional study, beginning with a modest art-college introductory course and concluding in the most prestigious art academy in Britain, he has emerged as an innovative and powerful artist. But as a small child he had difficulty in learning to speak, in writing and in relating to other people. Only his precocious drawing skills revealed to the more receptive individuals around him that his disabilities of that time masked considerable potential.

Becoming an artist was for him a difficult journey, longer and more of a struggle than for most of his contemporaries; he had to cope with the social and educational problems which unusual children encounter and to mature in spite of them. It has been a journey remarkable for the continuity of his drawing impulse and the way in which he sustained it while it sustained him. His numerous drawings over the years reveal this interdependent relationship and how the will to succeed as an artist grew from the activity.

David's drawing history highlights some issues about artistic development which are obscure in otherwise similar studies. Are his initial impediments and later triumphs irrelevant to the experience of others? Or are they dramatic and daunting extensions of difficulties which apply to the lives and conditions of many?

David is the fourth of five siblings and the second of three sons. His parents lived for a time in what was then Rhodesia before settling in Suffolk. Although they are not professional artists, art is important to them, attracting them to galleries as well as helping in their understanding of David's achievements. His mother is an amateur painter; an uncle of hers, John Lewis Stant (1903–65), was a professional artist.

Suffolk is a county of England not that far from London, but one which seems comparatively remote and underpopulated. The countryside is flat, with large open fields interspersed with small villages, each with its own church tower to betray its position among the trees.

The family home in which David grew up fulfils the ultimate English idyll of a long, low and ancient steep-roofed cottage, surrounded by trees and flowers in a deep country garden; there were always domestic animals, including a cow and various dogs and cats. Village shops and a church, schools and inns are not far away, but the house is set in its own burgeoning organic world. Half a mile distant, an unprepossessing filling station supplies fuel to motorists on a fast and straight arterial road. The nearest city, Cambridge, is an hour's drive to the west.

David's first drawing impulse was a consequence of his difficulties with speaking. When it became apparent, by the time he was three and a half years old, that he was not learning to talk, one of the strategies his parents devised for helping him was to encourage as much drawing as possible. He seemed eager to draw, but his progress in speech was still slow; he appeared unmotivated, even resistant. He would often sit in the centre of the lawn clutching a toy but isolated from the rest of the family. Though socially unhelpful, his mother feels this gave him time to look around on his own and so he had less need to copy like other children. But there were occasions when he was more forthcoming: before he was four he displayed a surprising ability to tease his father, an essentially interactive skill which may have signified the beginning of a struggle on David's part to emerge from isolation. Sometimes too he would pull his mother around the house, emitting strange noises (even after he had begun to talk).

The prognosis for David's development could not at the time have seemed encouraging. The family doctor judged the child retarded and seemed to think help not worthwhile. Within the family, autism was tentatively mentioned (by David's perceptive grandmother) and discussed, but it was regarded at the time as unlikely. His own hindsight diagnosis, having seen the problem from within at the time, is that he had suffered from a condition rather like a stroke, where some areas of the brain or the mind develop and function more slowly than others: 'Your life is then negotiated by the strongest area of the mind, in my case the observational. This can be of an incredible detriment to normal learning … [and this is where] the concept of obsession comes in.'[1]

Well before he could talk it was obvious that he had a burning interest in pictures in other people's houses, including calendars, so much so that he soon possessed a huge collection of calendars given to him by family friends. This had longer-term consequences in the hoarding of postcard reproductions of paintings, which created an enduring interest in the work of the English painters: Constable, Turner and the lesser Atkinson Grimshaw.

The family made a concerted effort to encourage David to speak. They devised games, using animal picture cards ('Where is the pig?') and giving him 'dolly mixtures' (small sweets) as prizes, although he soon enjoyed the games for themselves. He received a lot of attention in such ways and it is not surprising that at least one of the other children remembers feeling a twinge of jealousy because of that, though in the longer term relationships among the siblings have been good.

Undoubtedly the language campaign was crucial, a rescue action from a condition that might otherwise have intensified. Speech came slowly, as though gradually released. Drawing too emerged as a regular and enthusiastic activity from four and a half years. These earliest drawings were surprisingly and explicitly representational; when David was nearly five he made an identifiable image of a particular local church (fig.9.1) and greatly astonished the district nurse who happened on one of her visits to see him making it. This spontaneous drawing, in 'biro' pen, effectively recalls the solid strength as well as the detail of the tower and nave. It is one of the first of what was to become a constant stream of reportage by David on the nature and character of his own part of the Suffolk landscape. Like his numerous other drawings of the time, it is delicately small and wavering in line.

David's drawings of this period are not only remarkable because they are effectively representational, but also because many of them are actually compositions,

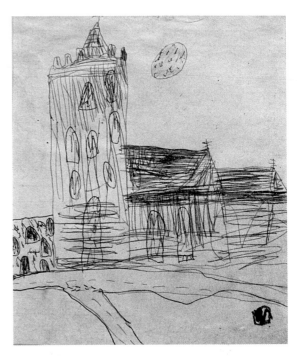

9.1 David Downes, *Eye Church*, 1975 (age 4)

in which buildings are clustered together, sometimes with trees and under clouds (see, for example, fig.9.2). Unlike most children, who at that age portray single or visually unrelated objects, he was already assembling his visual components into whole pictures.

From the intimate nature of these works, they appear to have been self-generated rather than bidden by his anxious family. But it is impossible to say whether so much drawing would have taken place if David had not been encouraged. From the distance of time it appears that he was diffusing inner anxieties as well as drawing from his surroundings for these images. Later he wrote, 'What consumed me was my overwhelming desire to draw, and to express my emotions. The drawings did not convey isolation, they more communicated a desire to be swallowed up by this imaginary world.[2]

That world was for him perplexing and alarming. He was always fascinated by weather conditions as well as frightened by bad weather in all its forms. He was made especially uneasy by the similarity between the forms of some quite harmless objects and their visual meteorological counterparts. A bare-branched tree could be very worrying because it resembled lightning. Cracks in masonry (perhaps for the same reason) had the same effect and would cause him to stare in horror at them, once frightening his younger

9.2 David Downes, *Church scene*, 1978 (age 6)

9.3 David Downes, *Windmill*, 1977 (age 6)

brother with the intensity of his gaze. He was abnormally afraid of low-flying aircraft; in that part of
England, fighter aircraft undertook regular training.
David remembers how he found them grotesque and
the noise intolerable; he would scream loudly as they
passed over. Possibly most alarming of all to him were
windmills, of which there were several derelict ones in
the area (fig.9.3). Of one in particular on the coast near
Southwold, he later wrote that 'The prevailing winds
and decades of desertion had sculpted it into a very
twisted shape. I could not get within yards of it
without bursting into hysterical fits of fear.'[3] He also
responded to fears of the unseen; he was terrified
when he heard, for instance, of a man who had met
a violent death in a nearby mill, having been trapped
in the blades. Thus the drawings which feature trees,

9.4 David Downes, *Village, tree and bird*, 1976 (age 5)

9.5a David Downes, *Church and road junction*, 1977 (age 6)

storms, lightning, clouds, broken walls, aircraft and windmills were not only stimulated by the simple sight of what was around him in the Suffolk countryside but also, and even mainly, by an instinctive desire to diffuse their threatening aspects. To achieve this he had to make them look 'scary' and to incorporate in them the shapes and forms which he found (he says) so 'horribly grotesque' (fig.9.4).[4]

Not all the things which fascinated him were terrifying; some were persistently intriguing places, observed on journeys by car to towns and villages in the area. Constantly intriguing were large churches situated at the junction of several roads, which seemed to him to be oddly in the middle of nowhere. Road junctions, signposts and road-markings, the bends in the roads and the various routes between places, became major obsessions as features of numerous drawings (he had a fascination for electricity pylons too, but oddly he never drew them). All these features were drawn from memory, in character and in detail, entering into his larger imagination as they grew. He now marvels at the way you can look at some of these drawings and

feel you could turn a corner in a road or around a building (for example, figs 9.5a and b).

Early on, David's sense of intrigue with places seen and remembered led to the imagining and portrayal of places unseen; often these were constructed by an amalgamation of several real places into one imagined one. Thus was invented 'Trottingham' – the name was created at the same time as the drawing, possibly combining the real Birmingham and Nottingham, although he had only seen the first. The big city must have been startling at first, to a small boy growing up in the country; he avidly drew impressions of huge high buildings and ravelled motorways as well as of the smaller and older houses nestling in their shadows. These are highly detailed cityscapes, with an infinity of tiny bricks and tiles, windows, people and vehicles (and an occasional out-of-place windmill), expressing his intense and passionate vision.

One other motivating idea seems crucial, the notion of power. David now remembers that he had always been attracted to powerful things. He feels that he never wanted the power for himself; it was merely the idea of it which was exciting. There was evident power in the lightning he feared, but it was also implicit in the towers of churches and tall buildings. Especial power could be found in the animate, even when not directly encountered: 'I had these lion books for Christmas. I hadn't seen lions before; they were fierce and powerful.' There was power too in people, perhaps too much to accommodate easily at times: 'Uncle John was very grumpy, so I thought I would personify him as a lion', and he drew him disproportionately large and roaming fiercely across his bedroom (see fig.9.6). Through drawing, he courted the destructive power

9.5b David Downes, *Costa del Sol*, 1984 (age 13)

9.6 David Downes, *Uncle John as a lion*, 1977 (age 6)

visible in the demolitions which he sometimes witnessed; he remembers his fear of 'cranes with balls on the end, smashing buildings up to build skyscrapers that looked even worse' and although he says he wasn't enjoying the damage, there was perhaps some of the usual boy's enjoyment of drama, danger and violence along with the anxiety engendered by it.

The family's joint effort to develop David's speech skills was eventually successful, and from then on he began to revel in talking, in the longer term paradoxically developing a taste for excitable discourse as well as the kind of sharp ear for the sound of it which makes for a good mimic. Other difficulties were not so soon overcome. At his nursery school he would respond diffidently to other children and would often sit in a ditch beside the playground rather than join in the games. His behaviour in class was awkward; some teachers found it difficult to be sufficiently sympathetic towards him, failing to understand that his problems were rarely of his own making. Some explanations for his curious behaviour have emerged more recently. For instance, when he was at nursery school he would often hang his head sideways. His mother now believes that he was in fact trying to get a better view of Eye church tower through the window, which along with other towers deeply attracted him and became the subject of many drawings.

There were many such obsessions. He was fascinated by clocks and watches, grabbing them and reading their numbers eagerly. His highly retentive visual memory, evident in so many of his early drawings, was matched by a remarkable facility with remembered numbers, even though he was slow to learn times tables. This eclectic memory was ably demonstrated in later adolescence when he would relay an entire sports result list in every detail from the television screen to his father who was working at the end of the garden. His memory too for things said and their occasions has always been astonishing. His least successful efforts were attempts to work in three dimensions; he felt an overwhelming need to make a weathervane out of cardboard, as part of coming to terms with the weather. In this he frustrated himself, failing to anticipate the effects of the weather itself upon cardboard. When his father finally bought him a weathervane, David felt a great sense of release from the failure.

Unusual skills are not always valued at school. They may pass unnoticed because teachers do not expect to see them, particularly in a child with learning or behavioural problems; they may be deemed irrelevant to the curriculum. Such a child may conceal special skills in an attempt to appear more like other children. Although some of David's primary-school teachers

respected him and noticed his unusual drawing ability, its significance was rarely recognized. He was judged an awkward pupil, apparently inattentive and slow to understand what he was expected to do. Meanwhile his mother had begun saving his drawings because, she says:

I thought it was unusual for a child not to copy, and [only] to draw from memory. He never used a rubber and drew straight away with a pen. My other children were fairly artistic but David was quite different in the way he executed a picture. I think the way he draws has a great deal of relevance. It has answered questions as to why he got poor reactions for so much of his work. He relied too much on his visual memory and didn't research.

By the time he was six, David's speech development was still not advanced enough to avoid his allocation to the school's special class, where he could be given extra assistance. This separation affected his image with teachers for many years to come. He was aware too of his own coordination difficulties and embarrassed to take part in physical class activities. To cope with a largely unsympathetic environment where ridicule was constant, he retreated into drawing, with felt-tip pens, mostly windmills and churches. He was sometimes asked to draw and the results were often admired both by teachers and children, but he never felt he was understood as a person. Positive encouragement was plentiful and constant at home, on the other hand. He invented a character for himself called 'Henry Williamson', whose own home-made art cards could be exchanged for any real ones that David's mother and grandmother might be persuaded to provide.

Recollecting the classroom difficulties he encountered at around seven years, he describes a teacher who was frustrated with him because her instructions to him needed repetition. He explains this now as his own difficulty in understanding her, but recognizes that when another more intimidating teacher refused to repeat himself, 'I listened to him and got the instructions right.' But he could not escape from the teachers' low expectations of him. He resembled other children with learning difficulties, although he must have been different from most.

A drawing of another wrathful teacher (fig.9.7) shows his capability for composition and for conveying emotion. Mrs Kemp's face is flushed; we know this from the parallel lines across her cheeks, a device David may have learned from comic-book illustrations, though no one remembers him having access to comics, nor do his drawings generally suggest such a influence. Mrs Kemp is gazing fixedly at the artist so that we, as viewers, share his alarm, as we do with the claustrophobic imagery of 'Trottingham'.

9.7 David Downes, *Mrs Kemp, when she was angry*, 1978
(age 7)

It may be that David at this time was obsessed less
with the act of drawing than with the need to come to
terms with the demonic experiences which made him
so afraid. Certainly he quickly lost interest in some
drawings and needed prompting to finish them. The
act of drawing was more an act of withdrawing from
his immediate fears about people, school, places and
events. He pinned them down on his paper beneath his
hand, thus achieving symbolic control. The drawings
of windmills, cities and wild weather conditions,
particularly, were, as he recollects, 'the only source
of security in an insecure world'.

Some less trauma-induced subjects, conversely, re-
assured him of the security of family life. Drawings of
the half-timbered small-windowed house in its deep
and ever-growing garden, of family pets sprawled at
rest (fig.9.8), of views across fields to distant villages,
are all eloquent and tranquil expressions of a warmer
world. When he was nine years old, and partly
because he possessed a book about them which he
enjoyed with his grandmother, he made a series of

9.8 David Downes, *Two dogs resting*, 1980 (age 9)

9.9 David Downes, *Burning building*, 1982 (age 11)

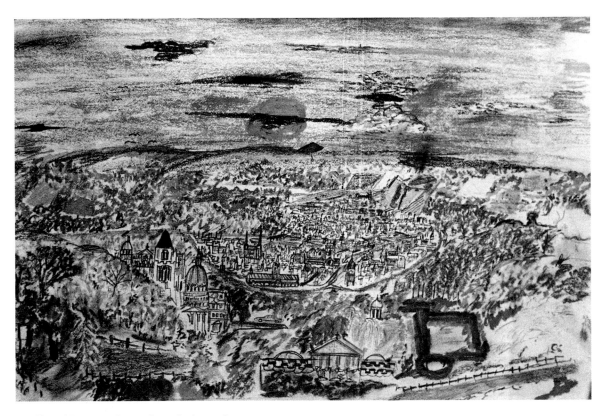

9.10 David Downes, *Dense city*, 1983 (age 12)

studies of birds. Whether in pencil, biro or crayon, these drawings show a fine awareness of the character of different creatures and are more evocative of their nature than the original photographs.

Human beings received less attention, with, for example, an occasional head-and-shoulders view of his father or where a local workman forms part of a scene. He began to experiment with charcoal (a medium which he was to use freely later, as a student), producing an unusual sketch based on a photograph of an abbey on the edge of cliffs. Books and photographs generally were very stimulating, providing ideas too at this time for a series of drawings on wars and battles.

The principal themes of earlier drawings – broad climatic country landscapes and dense architectural clustering – continued to appear in David's tenth, eleventh and twelfth years, at the time of his final year at primary school and first secondary years. Although some colour-crayon sketches of this period are loosely executed, generally the detail, either in pen or pencil, is intense. Even in a distant view across fields, he added minute details of foliage, towers, windows or the textures of clouds. Light, atmosphere and movement

are becoming important: previously static landscapes become transient events, seasonal as in *January snow, February floods* or *March gales*, or momentary as in pictures of the setting sun or of a fire (see fig.9.9). Sometimes these features take on a decorative aspect, where clouds or windows form an exotic and varying pattern. More human figures appear, mildly caricaturing rural life with their braces, pipes, beards or cricket bats and populating the village scenes like actors on a stage. Occasionally the fine detail of a cityscape is enriched by texture and colour (as in fig.9.10).

Even when some sketches, such as those made in Scotland in 1981 when David was ten, seem to have been directly observed, most are known to be from memory. At around this time, he was taken to the National Gallery in London, having asked to see the large Constable paintings there. For some years he had identified himself with that English painter, sharing his preoccupation with landscape as well as inhabiting the same English county, Suffolk. By the age of eight he had successfully, if simply, imitated Constable's and Turner's work with sensitive colour sketches (fig.9.11). His enthusiasm for Constable seemed, however, to

9.11 David Downes, *'I was interested in Turner'*, 1978 (age 7)

evaporate as he entered the Constable room in the Gallery and made for the centre seat, with no more than the briefest glance at what was on the walls. Seated, he hung his head and enquired about lunch. Subsequently it became clear from conversations and drawings that he had absorbed in a few seconds what other people take half an hour or more to see and that he could retain these observations indefinitely.

At his secondary school, social problems emerged again, this time not just in the form of loneliness and ridicule but also physical threats from bigger boys who were intolerant of anyone unusual. He made many attempts to integrate and to imitate, without much success. Sometimes these efforts only led to trouble with teachers; the problems of lack of dexterity which had dogged him from infancy (he had never been much good at ball games) caused innocent attempts at play to look like assault. Frustrated by being misunderstood, his general behaviour deteriorated, and teachers regarded him as uncooperative. Once again he found himself trapped in a class for pupils viewed as of poor potential, therefore obtaining neither an adequate education nor real help.

David had by this time realized that his skill at drawing was his greatest asset. But in the school art-room where he should have been able to flourish and reveal his strengths, he seems, judging by the drawings from that time, to have found that the work was alien to his own inclinations and to his already extensive personal repertoire. He made some occasional strong attempts to oblige his teacher, but his heart was not in the tasks he was assigned. His spontaneous drawings probably seemed too obsessively repetitive and his teacher no doubt wanted him to diversify. But the observational studies he drew (such as the art-room, its furniture and contents, or found objects such as shells, crushed cans or a coat) look lacklustre even when they are highly accomplished, without the fervour and individuality of the drawings he did concurrently at home (for example, *Hares in a field*, fig.9.12).

He admits that he was uncooperatively selective about what he was prepared to do, pursuing his own ideas and his obsession with only two major artists, Constable and Turner, to the exclusion of a more investigative attitude; his teacher left him increasingly

9.12 David Downes, *Hares in a field*, 1984 (age 13)

alone. At home, he began to focus on the dramatic portrayal of events in the Second World War in Europe as well as continuing his passion for the weather in all its alarming manifestations.

Sometimes there were occasions when his imagination was engaged by an idea proposed at school and his instinct for expression took over. Once he became fascinated by the idea of reflection, but used it to say something about the human condition through two associated portrayals of dereliction in the two halves of a drawing: 'I was trying to *reflect* the difference between severe adversity, a Northern miner with barely enough money to feed his family, and the Western front during the war.' These forays into symbolic compassion did not impress his teacher, who thought them to be subjects beyond David's understanding, taking a similar view of his interest in the Surrealist images of Dali.

In mid-adolescence, this developing concern for the meaning of images was matched by a growing awareness of the sensuality of the materials available to him, together with grasping the essence of a subject. At fourteen he made a poignant portrait in pencil of his

dying grandmother and a year later, in school, a remarkable profile study in pastel of a classmate (fig.9.13). Both are intense observations: the former linearly direct, the latter exquisitely coloured. So acute an eye for character and feeling seems to deny the existence of the problem of social interaction which had affected him so much, as well as the 'mental wilderness' which he felt he inhabited and from which he hoped so desperately to emerge.

The progress of David's drawing activities continued unabated, usually different in kind from his work in school. The spontaneous drawings generally remained small in scale, with much the same subjects as before, and similar texture and detail; they are often intricate and vigorous, revealing that he used a pen with aplomb. Evidently he handled drawing materials well, although his mother remembers him as frequently being clumsy and spilling things over other work. There was progress in the eloquence of his ideas and in the discovery, rehearsal and perfection of new techniques.

Around the age of twelve, for instance, the realization had come to David of the compositional potential

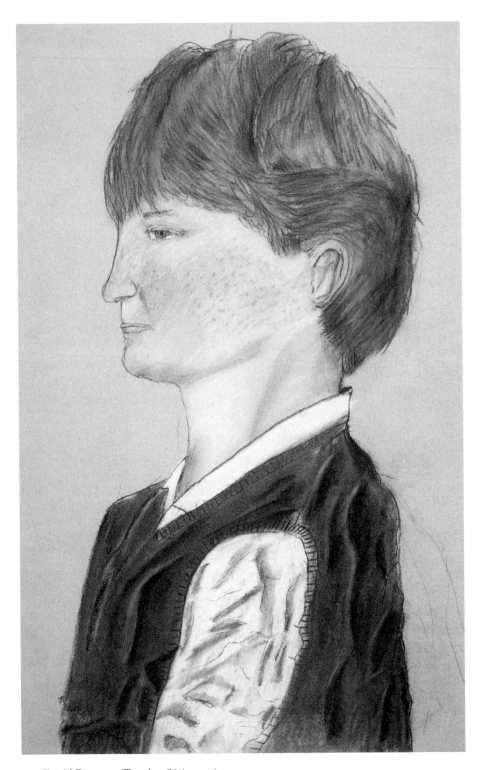

9.13 David Downes, *'Terry'*, 1986 (age 15)

9.14 David Downes, *Fox and tombstone*, 1986 (age 15)

in manipulating foregrounds. He had noticed that in fields at the height of summer, nearer, visually larger, growth provided a screen through which distant crops, trees or skies could be viewed. He made many drawings in which he explored this phenomenon. Similarly he realized that some of his separate studies of birds and animals might be integrated with landscape views to provide foreground detail or a focal point (an idea derived from the advice of his art teacher, originally directed to some of his schoolwork). From this idea came a series of strong drawings in which a fox, hare or partridge, drawn large and close even though partially hidden by foliage, provide the focal interest for increasingly lively and sophisticated drawings, such as *Fox and tombstone* (fig.9.14). He studied stuffed animals at school and applied this knowledge, as in *Peregrine falcon* (pl.VIII); the family calf became the ultimate foreground bridge between landscape and portrait in an empathetic colour study.

In spite of these difficulties at school, including those in the art-room, the idea of a career in art for David had grown steadily at home, where he had always felt protected and where both his difficulties and remark-able abilities were respected. His mother had entered some of his drawings in occasional competitions, but it is doubtful whether their authenticity, in terms of the age of the artist, was accepted. At school he had struggled to conform to the demands of art examinations; a preparatory sketch for an exam at fifteen shows how inhibited he became under stress – drawing a figure sketching in a village, he left the form inside the figure blank, happier to concentrate on the architecture, even though earlier drawings show how competent he actually was with such subjects. Nevertheless, by the age of sixteen he had amassed an exceptionally large and individualistic portfolio of work.

He left his secondary school to take up a place at Ipswich Art College in Suffolk, where he was offered the opportunity of a general Art and Design diploma course, even though he did not have the usual number of school examination pass grades. Here he found some sympathetic tutors whose value to him lay in understanding his need to develop new visual, expressive and practical skills, working through rather than against the skills and ideas which David had already formed. He was encouraged to reinterpret

9.15 David Downes, *Church at sunset*, 1987 (age 16)

9.16 David Downes, *Reclining nude*, 1988 (age 17)

9.17 David Downes, *Dark avenue*, 1988 (age 17)

some of his most intimate personal themes by changing their scale and adopting new media and techniques. Thus he discovered the liquidity and flow of the watercolour medium in addition to inks and pastels. He worked several times larger than was his custom, painting new images of the Suffolk fields and churches (see, for example, fig.9.15). He learned to draw using different devices such as cut sticks. New subject-matter was gradually introduced; he discovered the life-room and how the sensuality of medium and form could blend together, as in *Reclining nude* (fig.9.16). In this friendly environment, he was better able to cope with examination drawings too.

At seventeen, the taught and spontaneous threads of David's work began to unite, as a study of an avenue of lime trees, *Dark avenue*, reveals (fig.9.17). Painted on location, deploying his new-found techniques and evocative of the dark mysticism of the nineteenth-century English artist Samuel Palmer, it records a place which had affected him emotionally.

David's introductory year at Ipswich was followed by a further two years on an illustration course in Cambridge. Unfortunately, this course was not awarded degree status during the time he was there,

but it did provide further experience which he needed, with a good grounding in drawing and in illustration design. At the end of it, and because of the acute employment difficulties which beset the whole country at the time, he was unsure what to do next. A brief study visit to Portugal during the Cambridge course produced a series of newly vibrant colour studies which show aptitude as a painter, with feeling for the iconology of the image itself as well as for the subject of the study. With this new work and the credibility of his diploma studies he found he was acceptable for a higher degree course in the art college at Brighton; he arrived there in 1992 in his twenty-first year.

While it brought him into contact with lively tutoring, the Brighton course also involved problems which affected him even more than others. It was part-time and at first the students were obliged to work in their own accommodation on four out of five weekdays, with only one full day working together with tutors in the college. He needed more of this contact and only his dedication enabled him to keep going until tutor–student contact was increased.

His tutors encouraged him to develop a structured drawing project. He made a considerable number of portrait studies of the elderly residents of a nursing home, which reveal him once again as an exceptionally sensitive and perceptive portraitist. In 1993 he challenged himself to go to Madrid alone for three weeks. There he relished the novelty of a different landscape and atmosphere. He rediscovered, in a new setting, the high buildings which had awed and threatened him in childhood. Finding them no longer alarming but still exciting, he made rapid studies of the canyoned older streets and their inhabitants. These drawings, often etched heavily into the paper, show his determination to grasp the rich visual opportunity afforded him. On a visit two years later to Italy, he chose the same subject-matter but this time the drawings are more confident and subtle, more sensitive to the materials and more provocatively animated by his observations.

David was emerging as an outwardly more confident individual, passionate about his profession, eagerly grasping advice from tutors and living excitedly through every project. Inwardly, he remained anxious about himself. From being in early childhood so isolated from others, he had developed from late adolescence into a paradoxically gregarious person, thriving on contacts with family and friends; he became talkative, interesting and entertaining. Some problems remained: keen to make peer friendships, he was perhaps too positive in doing so, sometimes provoking adverse reactions from those who found him unpredictable.

The opportunity to apply for further study at the

9.18 David Downes, *Great windmills*, 1993 (detail)

prestigious Royal College of Art in London was not to be missed. It says much for the expert guidance of the tutors of all three of his previous study institutions, as well as for the remarkable depth of his own endeavours, that he was now equipped with enough experience and examples of work to be offered a place.

In spite of his flair and dedication in early years, David's psychological journey, beginning with so many disadvantages, has been an arduous one, though he has been so well assisted by his concerned and supportive family. In the final phase of his Brighton course, David was asked to submit a written and illustrated dissertation; he chose to record the path of his early 'Disordered Development'.[5] The drawings illustrating this penetrating account are lusty, graphic and painful evocations of his early fears of objects, phenomena and especially people, those who made his life so alarming at school. Among the dynamic graphite works illustrating the text is one featuring, across a double-page spread, an irregular line of massive windmills, with their sails dominating the moving sky and their bases embedded in a sea of windswept grasses; a small human figure stares up at them. These structures, recurrent throughout the whole of the artist's drawing development from the age of four, are now presented as dramatic robots straddling the landscape, still alarming but also somehow defiant and triumphant emblems of the journey and its conquests (see *Great windmills*, fig.9.18).

The full extent of David Downes's achievement as a mature professional artist remains to be seen. He has studied alongside the most able of art students and in the footsteps of the eminent: Henry Moore, David Hockney and others who achieved international status during their lifetimes. Whatever his ultimate achievement, it cannot now be insignificant and, in the light of his history, it is already remarkable.

10

Sustaining expression through drawing

When I enter the chapel [at Vence], I feel that the whole of me is there ... I mean everything that was best in me when I was a child, and which I have tried to preserve all through my life.

Matisse

The examples of the seven artists featured in this book (and the details from the lives of many others) serve to shed light upon some significant issues which broader analytical studies cannot illuminate, such as what might be the events which trigger artistic activity, the intentions underpinning it in different circumstances and the effects of tuition or contact with art. Their differences include nationality, century or decade of birth, gender, cultural and social background, family life-style, parental involvement with art, physique, personality, education, development, professional objectives and, most importantly, subject-matter, style and meaning in their work. These differences are helpfully interesting in themselves, but also render any common experiences or achievements particularly significant in relation to them.

That evidence is rarely unequivocal; it is not always easy, for instance, to distinguish cause from effect; we cannot always know whether archives may be short of key works; artists and their biographers may have been misquoted. No hard theory about artistic development can emerge from such circumstances (not that this has deterred others in the past). The study confirms that development in drawing fluency, particularly when obsessively led, cannot be reduced to a common formula, as some would have it; individuality is the ultimate and wonderful reality. There are nevertheless some intriguingly similar features in these seven accounts.

The obsession

Common to all the seven artists (as well as to others) is the early manifestation of an obsession to draw. What-
ever their peers were doing around them at the same age, these individuals strove endlessly to make drawings from seductive ideas and were clearly deeply engrossed in their making, sometimes responding to external influences but often seeming to be impelled from within.

Apart from Millais, perhaps, they were all early independent thinkers (even if they were inhibited in other respects), quick to pick up nuances and inferences, inventive and flexibly minded. The influence of other children's drawings seems to be non-existent or short-lived, taken up exploitively only by some at a key moment, but quickly discarded. Where adults imposed ideas and traditions upon any of them, some, possibly secretive, way was found to sustain a parallel but idiosyncratic activity that was at least as important as the overt.

None of the seven were easily deflected from their endeavours, any more than Michelangelo was by his disapproving father. If they did not draw illicitly in their schoolbooks (and we know that several did), they readily improvised in circumstances that others might have found limiting. Ideas were stimulated by unusual (even awkward) sizes or proportions of the paper available. The range of available materials seems to have been unimportant; while many young artists describe, like Tom Phillips, the intoxicating nature of certain kinds of paints, inks or dry media, any available materials would be adapted for expressive effect, while the artists preserved what mattered to themselves. The impetus derived from this obsession functioned both to strengthen and to protect; continuing practice made for increasing invention and flexibility.

Their obsession enabled all seven eventually to emerge as artists. However, there are other instances where it was not enough – it was not strong enough in 'Peter' for instance (discussed in Chapter 2, p.19), to protect the activity from his increasingly damaged self-image, or in the case of Stephen Wiltshire to save it from an insufficiently maturing personality.

We do not know whether late-developing artists such as Alfred Wallis have been this obsessive in childhood. The possibility is that they were not, or they might have found some way at the time to circumvent their unhelpful circumstances. An obsession can perhaps lie dormant for some time or develop slowly over years, awaiting sufficient strength or a trigger event.

The extreme depth of the initial obsession is a common phenomenon in those who become artists of all kinds, and not just in the highest achievers, but only in its strongest manifestations might it be considered as predictive of achievement, otherwise being vulnerable to deflection. Sustaining the obsession powerfully seems essential to ultimate high performance, and if it should cease at any time, eventual high attainment seems unlikely. A high volume of drawing activity seems crucial to the quality of the ultimate achievement and also, apparently, to its effectiveness in interaction with personal development.

Because it can appear very early, this obsessive inclination may be innate, although no one can be sure of that. But it can also be generated, as both education and the cases of late-developing artists show, and therefore it can be cultivated, too, and lead to a confident commitment to consequent activity, in more people than only those who initially display it.

Progression

It is hardly surprising when such intensive and sustained activity as we have seen leads to the unusually rapid development of drawing skills and interests. Every mature artist recognizes the huge investment in time and experiment required to generate real progress as an artist; without it, there is constant regression and insufficient impetus for development. Children exhibit much the same difficulty as they journey towards and through adolescence.

While the mythology that there is such a thing as a gift or a talent for drawing and art suggests that exceptional children ought to be able to draw and paint effortlessly from the beginning, the records here show intense and persistent endeavour, matching that of the mature artist in overcoming difficulties and perfecting techniques. Some drawings appear to have been easily accomplished, but there are also sequences of obvious rehearsal, repetition, adjustment and struggle, such as Hoffnung's infant experiments with the geometry of heads and Sarah Raphael's constant re-improvisations of social scenes as sequential story sketches.

One can see why less motivated children might adopt the simple formulae for drawing which they see other children using. Even four of our seven artists passed through such stages, although not for long. Two others, born in the nineteenth century and at first educated separately from children beyond the family (Millais at eight and Lautrec from twelve years), appear not to have used these shared systems. Nor did David Downes at any stage, who appears to have had no need of them or perhaps never to have noticed them.

Childhood schemata (the structures commonly used by children at an early stage to express visual concepts) are no twentieth-century phenomenon. Giovanni Francesco Caroto's sixteenth-century portrait of a small boy with a figure-drawing constructed from boxes, parallels and a circle (now in the Museo di Castelvecchio, Verona), shows it to be earlier. If Millais and Lautrec passed through such a stage, it must have been before their work began to be saved. But there may have been no intervening phase between the earliest attempts at drawing (in the period so wrongly described as one of mere scribble and gesture) and later tutored academicism.

Much has been written about the alleged inevitability of the adolescent crisis and its consequences in the demise of drawing fluency, with a loss of interest in what was at an earlier stage for most individuals a compelling activity. The seven featured artists reveal no such problem; even David Downes, who was bewildered by periods of unhelpful teaching, simply continued his most important investigations at home.

Whether or not the compulsion to draw was sustained, for the exceptional individuals, seems to have depended upon the sheer diversity of the intense drawing experiments they had undertaken prior to adolescence; their fervour and tenacity had made them searching, ingenious and eclectic. Millais conformed at the Academy but improvised when away from it; Picasso observed, imagined, copied and borrowed; Rothenstein played with visual effects; Hoffnung persevered with countless ways of expressing the same themes. Like extremely well-rehearsed actors, they were less likely to be overwhelmed later by the pressures of an audience or a convention upon their performance, having a repertoire of skills, styles, techniques and subject-matters for almost any situation.

All seven were soon aware that different styles of drawing could be effective for the expression of different ideas. They knew that if you constructed a drawing differently, or used different kinds of lines or shadings, you could give it other meanings, making a surface hard, soft, smooth or rough, causing something to appear to be moving, or a scene to be romantic, sad or funny. They were quick to absorb the qualities of images around them, whether family paintings or photographs, or illustrations in children's books. Hoffnung and Lautrec transposed the style of illustrators with whom they were familiar into their own style, early enough to suggest it to be a subconscious act. Rothenstein in childhood was a good conscious imitator of style (as with the Indian miniatures), later picking up a style of caricature from contemporary magazines.

A familiarity with other art was something they all shared, with Downes providing the most explicit evidence of this in his attempts to *be* Constable or Turner. For Millais this relationship began with the lesser works he was asked by his tutor to copy and then continued with a broad and probably casual acquaintance with conventional works, such as sporting paintings, owned by the family. His extremely early studentship at the Royal Academy Schools brought him into contact with major works in public collections. It is remarkable in these heavily prescribed circumstances that he integrated his own preoccupations with those of the works around him in such a way as to create a more personal artistic style than might otherwise have been the natural conclusion. Lautrec's introduction to art was similarly conservative, lacking a broader spectrum in spite of the new initiatives in French art of the time; this is not true of the two youngest artists in this study, surrounded as they were by discussion about art within the family.

Such influences, from wherever they were derived and however they were subsumed into the drawing experience, seem to have been important as part of the phenomenon of development, acting as bridges to further and eventually more independent phases. In Hoffnung's drawing sequences this is especially clear, as he moved from one technique or subject idea or style to another, holding on to each until new discoveries carried him further.

Intention

So far as is discernible from the available records, each of the seven artists had developed in the beginning a recognizable ambition for direct rather than formulaic representation. Popular opinion and previous educational theory usually presumes the earlier mark-making to be meaningless but the 'motor activity' or 'gestural scribble' in those years may be highly representational in intention, usually 'unreadable' only because of insufficient contextual reference.[1] The Millais, Lautrec and Picasso archives open between the ages of six and eight years with sketches so well observed (in their different forms) that a much earlier beginning to this activity seems probable. The Rothen-

stein, Hoffnung, Raphael and Downes collections all include such earlier sketches.

As a child, Millais was quickly put under pressure to learn and to achieve academic conformity, to adopt the techniques of formal representation and the conventions of the art of his time. But in his more spontaneous and natural sketches he shows that the tactile sensations of drawing, the tools and the surfaces, as well as his visual experience, are more expressive of inner feeling than might have been acceptable at the time. It is wonderful to consider this as an early-nineteenth-century piece of evidence for the expression of a child's naturally responsive 'naive vision', so envied a century later by Picasso and his contemporaries.

All seven artists show in their earliest work a natural affinity with materials and with the expression of feeling through them. Lautrec was more interested in the way the horses seemed to hurtle across the landscape than in their anatomical structure. Picasso paid early attention to his father's teaching, but expressed his own vitality through the materials. Hoffnung may have gone to the circus (like Lautrec); in drawing, he celebrated his own amusement in the comic potential of the situation beyond detailed observation.

Rothenstein recorded things around him but interspersed them with quite different drawings, in which the ideas are variously decorative, fantastic or brutal. Sarah Raphael too has a comic thread running through much of her earliest work, with an element of psychological investigation of encounters between individuals which also characterizes the interests of the young Hoffnung; hers are more autobiographical, his more symbolic. For David Downes, perhaps most of all, the drawings are expressive of feeling but also cathartic in diffusing its most uncomfortable aspects. Such an affective role for drawing, highlighted in his case, may have been common to the rest of the group, if less explicit in their cases. The images are talismanic, embodying the aspirations as well as the fears of their makers. Their creation and sometimes their continuing existence are important, as secure and triumphant bases for subsequent creative acts.

The obsession and the energy began, in all these cases, not as a drive to perform impersonally and to make images just like other people's, but as an interactive passion between individual and experience. Responding to encouragement (as they also mostly were) by quickly learning to imitate, they also sought opportunities to express what was most personal. Because their prime interest was in that way egocentric, they often explored the *possibilities* of things rather than the way they actually were, and drew them using personal rather than general methods.

How else may one explain Hoffnung's remarkable drawn 'essays' in visual comparison, his adaptations of the human form for different purposeful ends, or the fascinating shifts of approach to drawing the same subject-matter exhibited (and described retrospectively) by Rothenstein?

The intensity as well as the prolific nature of such independent drawing experiences, particularly *prior* to contact with the conventions perpetuated in schools or other social groups, may well further the impetus of highly motivated children to exploit but not to be overwhelmed by the conventions evident around them. Most extraordinarily, it seems to set up the expressive intention for many years to come and even for a whole lifetime of drawing. The so-early emergence and lifelong persistence of individual themes, such as Rothenstein's cockerels and butterflies or Hoffnung's body adaptations, is a remarkable revelation. With the passing of childhood and the transition through adolescence, the character of the spontaneous drawing changes, becoming variously structure-exploring, event-capturing, comic, fantasy-inventing, sensual, romantic, satirical or photographic in intention. These are represented in all the seven, but generally build on rather than displacing earlier themes.

The pace and path of development

Many theories about the development of drawing fluency adhere to the concept of an ideal pace, with deviations above and below that, according to 'talent' and tuition or 'early' or 'late' development. These ideas are supported by various historical attempts to envisage a distinct sequence of drawing development which can be itemized according to certain subject-matters, intentions or techniques; the most frequently adopted of these concerns the proportional representation of parts of a form (usually human), with a notion of degrees of 'accuracy' or 'correctness' implied as a condition for successful drawing at specific ages.[2] In her *The Right to Speak* (1992), with its interesting parallel meanings for learning to draw, Patsy Rodenberg points out that the 'right' does not imply that there is only one way to be expressive.[3] She stresses the mystical as well as the inhibiting nature of the concept of an ultimate ideal expressive mode.

The work of our seven artists poses problems in relation to these views of development; in their spontaneous early drawing they had different criteria for the making of many of their images. Given that the purpose of particular drawings was, for instance, to express movement (Lautrec, Picasso, Hoffnung), comedy (Rothenstein, Hoffnung, Raphael) or fear or

exhilaration (Rothenstein, Downes), their modes of portrayal of individual forms (human, animal or inanimate) relate to the nature of the idea. Millais' Dinant soldiers are fleetingly tentative; Sarah Raphael's human figures are more precise, grotesquely funny or powerfully observed; Rothenstein drew people differently in different drawings; Hoffnung drew different figures differently in the same drawing (fig.7.3). To attempt to determine the progressive stages represented in such drawings against rigid external criteria would produce some unsound judgements.

Except for Millais, all the other six artists were fascinated by movement – with figures running, falling or throwing and with objects propelled by various forces. Those born in the twentieth century took their techniques for doing this initially from the characteristics of drawings in comic-papers, distorting figures and objects so as to imply their weight and direction of movement as well as sometimes showing trajectories and impacts by the use of appropriate marks. Rousseau may have been right to argue that from such investigations in childhood we come to understand our place as beings in space, in time and in a world of other objects.[4] Again, too, the flexible thinking that is generated may help to sustain later drawing activity.

What are the most important kinds of drawing activities to nurture progress in these or any other individuals? Once formally tutored, the artists all learned quickly enough to draw in the cultural idiom of their day and place, with attention to detailed observation and employing conventions of line, tone, perspective and composition in order to represent objects spatially; these are perhaps the easiest features of training to become an artist. But in doing so they had (intuitively at least) to cherish those other aspects of drawing which had initially motivated their obsession: its capacity for the expression of their impressions, emotions, feelings and ideas. Each of the seven found his or her own way of achieving this, picking up different cues according to circumstances at the time and making greater or lesser leaps of understanding and practical competence. However great was their need to become expert in the accredited conventions, the initial enthusiasm for what drawings could be made to convey was continually explored, especially in numerous 'unofficial' works of importance to their young makers even if not to observers.

Collectively (and with regard also to other examples), the seven studies above show that judgements about levels or directions of development at any time are fraught with difficulty, precisely because the individuals are driven more by personal than imposed intentions; their 'pathways' are different too and certainly more complex than the linear models that have been proposed. If other less remarkable individuals fit such models, it is because their development is less powerfully autonomous, more vulnerable to diversion and to pleasing their mentors.

This is not to say that notions of progress and pace are irrelevant; it is, after all, the discovery that someone is drawing with sophistication much sooner than we normally expect that is an accepted if controversial sign of exceptional facility. But sophistication may take different forms; the drawing *The temptation* by the seven-year-old Hoffnung is not a noticeably strong one in visual, observational terms, but expressively and for a seven-year-old it is a tour-de-force of imagination in understanding the human predicament and, as such, highly sophisticated. In judgements of performance at any stage, our vision of what is significant needs to be sensitive to these many possible intentions.

Subjects, sources and meanings

The very early appearance of lifelong thematic interests we have seen is indeed startling. This is less apparent in the case of Millais, possibly because his formal tuition began so soon. Even here, however, his lifelong interest in and distinctive use of foliage makes an early appearance. With Lautrec it is the style of drawing in particular which endures into maturity, the power of his energetically racy line and its implication of movement for all it creates. Constantly rehearsed in childhood, these qualities are characteristic of his later observations, especially of dancers, drawn in motion or poised for it. Hoffnung's earliest life-themes were particularly enduring, in distortions of the human form or its occlusion with inanimate objects, in his analyses of humans as they encounter each other, in the obsession with musical instruments and of course with humour itself.

In spite of many later changes of style and the creation of completely new concepts of visual expression, Picasso often returned to the subject-matter of his childhood, the pigeons and portraits from his father's influence. Rothenstein eschewed his childhood obsession with the cruel and the bloody, but in his final years the cockerels and hens, insects, butterflies and to some extent the colour of the more pastoral side of his childhood work became increasingly prevalent again.

For Sarah Raphael, something monolithic about the kind of human-figure drawings that illustrate her childhood stories lives on in the figures of her sombre landscapes; but it is the sequential story-pictures of her adolescence which so powerfully recur in the *Strip* paintings of her later thirties. David Downes's first portrayals of churches, signposts and clouds are still features in his work; the drawings, now orchestrated by experience but still often richly detailed and textured, extend the images of those early days.

So early do these themes first appear in some cases that one can only speculate on their origins. A particular drawing style may derive simply from physical characteristics; in my study of twins, I have shown that the one with early dexterity problems was the one whose drawings later became more energized, flowing and less literal.[5] Hoffnung's focus on music as a seven-year-old may have been due to his mother; his humorous attitudes could have been inherited or developed as a consequence of infant experiences; his (not wholly humorous) fascination with redesigning the body cannot so easily be explained, although it is perhaps only a manifestation of thoughts we all have about the body's efficiency in a modern world.

The painter Alan Davie has commented that 'in childhood I used to draw snakes; I'm still drawing them!'[6] Of course in his mature paintings they are not snakes any more, and perhaps they never were; it is the 'snakeness' of snakes that appears in his otherwise abstracted compositions; the connection is there. Such long-term influences reveal just how important early drawing is and how damaging to expressive fluency the absence of such activity may be for others, whether or not they have a future in art.

Copying and the art context

Traditionally, copying from the works of other artists has been a reputable activity for an artist in training and sometimes also for an established artist; Picasso spent much time during his life studying the works of other artists in order to analyse their styles and methods. At some stage in their early drawing development, all the seven here engaged in copying activities. Millais and Lautrec copied from the Antique in their first years of formal art training; long before that stage, Millais was copying the paintings of minor artists. Picasso made copies of pictures in his home that were by his father; Rothenstein made loose copies of his father's purchased miniatures; and Downes made copies from memory or invented his own versions of his favourite Turner and Constable paintings. Such activity seems to have been instinctive, intended to fulfil at least two functions: to find useful ideas in the techniques and subject-matters of other artists and to gain understanding of the different genres of art.

Copying appears to have been useful, especially when the works studied were of high quality; otherwise, as with Millais, they tended to stultify rather than to inspire. Hoffnung did not copy directly but grasped at the styles of several illustrators before rejecting them all and developing his own; those that were rejected had played their part in successively advancing his own learning. This instinctive utilization of the work of established artists is clearly important to development generally.[7] It is, however, only instrumental and the ability to copy is not in itself a significant skill by which to detect the future artist; that role demands skills of imagination as well as strengths of character in the making of new images as opposed to the copying of old ones. Most of Rembrandt's students copied his style so closely that they failed to discover the essence of his works.

In his autobiography, W. P. Frith recalls how, as a successful Academician, he met the more senior fellow-Academician who had once approved his boyhood candidacy for studentship. When shown the very drawings (which were copies of other works) which had determined his judgement at the time, the older man was astonished at his own temerity in having accepted such inadequate evidence and ashamed to have done so.[8] One might see this instance as confirming the value of copying in the diagnosis of artistic potential, but other evidence shows that his shame was correctly felt; only by chance did the student chosen have appropriate strengths, and those were conventional more than inspirational.

Parental influence

Although other examples (see Chapter 2) show it not to be essential, all seven artists examined here received encouragement as children, growing up in families that were sensitive to art if not actually involved with it. They would have acquired some notion of its place in life and also opportunities to imitate styles and techniques. There are differences in the ways in which their enthusiasm was treated. While Picasso was tutored from an early age by an ambitious and dominant teacher-artist-parent, the abilities of Rothenstein and Raphael were indulged rather than put under pressure, an open situation which the young Picasso might have envied, even though his own deep determination generated a potently valuable reaction to his father's influence.

It is easy to sympathize with the painter Howard Hodgkin when he declared that growing up in a family 'where everyone thought they knew about art' was 'very difficult'.[9] That indeed was the ultimately destructive problem for 'Peter', discussed in Chapter 2, whose parents were actively ill-informed rather than knowledgeably dominant. One can also appreciate the positive value of living in an artistic family with artists as role-models. Practical help may be less valuable, though, than is a sense of being understood, as Sarah

Raphael was by her literary parents. It seems more important to be provided with space and time in which to work than to be intensively directed. In a supportive ambience without regimentation, flexible experimentation can occur.

Crystallizing events

The accounts of particular events which may have stimulated first major thrusts towards an art career are diverse and impressive. Whether momentary illuminating experiences or gradual discoveries, and whether practical about drawing and painting sensations or more about the vision and role of the artist, these seem to be genuine memories which may have been pivotally effective.

Even so, Picasso was already aflame with artistic ambition before he saw the adulation given to the monarch whom he thought to be an artist (see Chapter 5). And Rothenstein had more possibility of becoming an artist simply because several of his family had preceded him in that direction. The flowing paint on his teacher's brush may not have started Tom Phillips (who lacked any really supportive environment) on his path, but it simply served to confirm an intention which had already been formed (see Chapter 2).

These apparently crystallizing experiences were probably crucial to the mature individual (like Wilfred Owen or Alfred Wallis). But for the young and as yet not openly dedicated individual, they may simply act to confirm and legitimize an existing desire rather than triggering something new. Tom Phillips's infant classroom was after all full of children who were witnesses to the teacher's spectacular actions (see pl.II); only one witness, so far as we know, was permanently affected by them.

Self-image

Like many professionals, several of our group of seven saw themselves as artists from an early stage, a vision openly or tacitly encouraged by their parents which then acted as an encouraging prophecy. Picasso's attention-seeking drawing quickly became linked to his perception of what an artist could be. The early artistic diligence of Millais, Lautrec and Hoffnung was rewarded with further opportunities for drawing. It is easy to see how the first experience of feeling talented and admired can have such a strong effect upon self-image and can generate artistic ambition. (Female children who were so admired were less likely, until the twentieth century, to reach the same conclusion about their future, as Germaine Greer notes.[10]) Self-image emerges as a key factor in development, whether formed as an imitative or a defiant response or an independent conviction, but rarely from acquiescence to imposed ideas or attitudes.

Sarah Raphael did not foresee her own artistic career until mid-adolescence, although she had always understood what it meant to be an artist. Her drawings were admired from her infancy, though not seeming exceptional until she was about thirteen. They were prolific and she was obsessive about the activity of drawing, but the family encouraged in her a sense of future freedom combined with a strong message about the discipline necessary to any worthwhile career in the arts. David Downes clung to the activity of drawing as though to a lifeline, but the idea of becoming an artist only formed gradually in him as other possibilities seemed remote, while drawing retained its potency for him beyond all else.

The experience of 'Peter' (in Chapter 2) serves as a warning to parents and teachers. Being in any respect exceptional does not make one unique. But to be described as unique and a genius, especially in early adolescence, might be unbearable, leading to frustration of the obsession to make art and to its destruction.

Tuition and schooling

Positive tuition prior to the age of ten may be advantageous or damaging, depending upon its quality and the intentions of those who elect to provide it for any child. Millais' early tutoring by Mr Bessell may have affected the nature of his later work substantially. It aligned him with the spirit of the age in art but he had to combat its more restrictive aspects. Lautrec was more fortunate than Millais, since Mantoy was more sensitive than Bessell, encouraging, as the child's drawings show, a more adventurous approach to drawing.

The lack of a tutor can create problems arising from interference by misguided adults, acting as amateur tutors. This was not a problem for Hoffnung and Rothenstein, whose parents were either indulgent or absent. Both children learned informally about the arts, about visual art and artistic values but remained unpressured; in adolescence Rothenstein went sketching with his encouraging but non-dominant father.

All of the seven went on to be educated in art institutions, but at different ages: Millais at eight, Lautrec at twelve, Picasso at eleven, Hoffnung at sixteen, Rothenstein, Raphael and Downes not until eighteen years. Since the timing of positive teaching remains controversial (for all children), one may speculate on what might have been the consequences for the last four, had they been admitted to specialist teaching at an earlier age. One could argue that Hoffnung's adolescent years were wasted so far as an art training was concerned; at a time when he could have been enabled to perfect his techniques and to study excellence, he was merely killing time with unfocused sketching. Sarah Raphael too was misunderstood and frustrated at her secondary school, until she found a sympathetic teacher; the freedom he provided may not have been all she needed. And Downes's schooling was a succession of mismatches between his capabilities and how they were perceived by primary and secondary school teachers.

Where the nineteenth-century artists might have benefited from a more flexible approach to the study of drawing (and we have seen that Millais withheld himself protectively from some parts of the Academy's more inflexible tuition), those educated in the twentieth century might have profited from more directed study of it at an earlier age. It is unfortunate that in some countries an egalitarian view of education prior to age eighteen as the same for all has stood in the way of advanced specialist provision in art, even though it is accepted for drama, music, dance and sport. While all tuition carries the risk of being misapplied, the opportunity to be taught by good artists and to have more time to focus on art in late childhood and early adolescence could have prevented much of the frustration experienced during those years by Hoffnung, Raphael and Downes.

Personality

Contemporary theory rejects the separation of nature from nurture in favour of their inextricably interactive role in the developing personality. In such a view it is still reasonable to propose that there are some aspects of personality which characterize future artists and to argue that inheritance combines, positively or reactively, with circumstances in the development of such characteristics.

There are echoes in these seven artists, that can be inferred from their drawings, of many descriptions of the personality of exceptional individuals generally: indications of unusual memory skills, of obsessive behaviour and remarkable persistence, of social awkwardness, of behavioural difficulties in the family and at school, and so on. They each remained persistently active, undeterred by contrary advice, inadequate teaching or seductive alternatives. They all retained a visual and tactile sensitivity, apparently less easily sustained in most other people.

This was not just an engagement with the visual world but also with its other sensory associations. The act of drawing is a response to tactile and other sensations as well as to the visual and the imagined. While most people have such sensitivity in infancy, many are culturally induced to abandon it for talking, writing and conceptualizing, at the expense of the sensory. By inclination or training, and by individual dedication and practice, the artist retains that sensitivity, a feeling for the tools and materials of art as well as for the surfaces, forms and other dynamics of visual and imaginative experience.

The case of David Downes throws additional light on characteristics associated with developing expressively. His early physical, intellectual and social difficulties were accompanied by a strong visual awareness and memory. The development of his artistic skills may have been either cause or effect in overcoming his difficulties. At first he simply used his drawing activity to hide in his own imaginative world and to diffuse his darkest fears, but he believes that later it played a positive role in assisting his overall intellectual and social development. The exceptional ability in one area of skill which is so visible in many autistic and certain other children where it is manifested in drawing forms a puzzling connection between autist and artist. Downes's experience shows that there can be causal connections in either direction. In becoming an artist, he has succeeded in shedding the impediments of his autist-resemblant condition while retaining its positive and useful phenomena.

Downes is not the only one of the seven to display some early behaviour reminiscent of autism. The description of Pablo Ruiz Picasso's behaviour, particularly on first being sent to school, reveals similar obsessive, physical and sometimes disruptive responses to those exhibited by many autists at the same age. There are hints of such evidence too in the biography of Rothenstein as a child, including early reading difficulties. We saw earlier that Tom Phillips had a number obsession in childhood, which is still active. Coupled with examples from other artists, a connection between the behaviour of young artist and young autist seems surprisingly common.

It would be unreasonable to suggest that all artists start out as autists, even though artists and some autists share drawing fluency in childhood and even though the conventional signals of exceptionality or actual genius sometimes appear to be replicated in one or other of the extraordinary skills displayed by some autistic individuals. The condition of being an artist is anyway full of variations, as the examples here demonstrate. The spectacular displays of early drawing in some autists have been known to give way to a gradual decline of that and other skills, while abstract thinking hardly appears at all. Alternatively, such an individual may develop moderate skills of abstract

thinking and social interaction, but the drawing facility itself never emerges as genuine visual and artistic thinking; it remains a sparkling record of things seen and remembered but is never much of a comment upon them.

The fundamental difference between the autistic Stephen Wiltshire (see Chapter 2) and David Downes is that the latter's earliest work, though obsessively repetitive, was always expressive. Both drew architecture but David's churches and cities were always statements of how he perceived them: with fear, excitement or curiosity, subject to the vicissitudes of weather and ageing as well as his own heady imagination. Wiltshire's drawings are more impersonal: where people are shown in relation to architecture, some feeling for space and movement may be inferred and a delight in decorative and especially repetitive detail seems apparent, but mostly the drawings appear as notebook inventories of structure and detail rather than as celebrations of observations or imaginings. As a child David Downes ranged much more widely across the spectrum of drawing possibilities into human and animal portraiture, into incidents such as bonfires, storms and irate teachers as well as invented places and events; his repetitions were also reinterpretations.

The connections between artist and autist are rarely as clear as with the autist-resemblant David Downes. But more links may exist than has previously been supposed. Other artists can be found, in addition to those specifically mentioned here, who initially displayed early language difficulties, were number-obsessed, experienced physical problems and had social difficulties. It is inappropriate for this author to offer physiological explanations for autistic or autist-like behaviour. But one may imagine that a number of skills, including expression through drawing, have potential for development according to physical, intellectual and to some extent social circumstances. The autistic cases might confirm that these skills are present in all of us: some are revealed and developed to varying extents, some are apparent but declining and others are never on view. In the struggle to develop skills from a visual-expressive tendency which some autists and some artists share, this unusual behaviour, much concerned with a confused confrontation between knowledge and feeling, seems to surface.

In the majority of individuals, the initial drawing fluency of the young child may diminish because any early disposition towards sensation and feeling is not itself strong enough to withstand the cultural onslaught of a world of words and logic. The key link between autist and artist, manifested in drawing fluency, may be that both manage to sustain a powerful bias towards sensory experience for longer than others. The autist (except in rare cases like that of Downes) cannot usually take this any further. Others have the necessary, if tacit, understanding to turn drawing into art, linking sensory experience with the human condition. And that is something that is open to the processes of education.

Distinguishing the future artist

Judgements of what is exceptional in drawing are frequently confused by limited expectations, recognizing only the traditional view. Early ability in terms of visual reportage, proportion, perspective, occlusion and detail, or simply a good, neat finish to a drawing, are, in Western cultures at least, noticed, prized and encouraged, while an untidy vigour and eloquent graphic invention can be undervalued or ignored. The dilemma of tradition versus individuality and expression is captured in the writings of the nineteenth-century English artist-historian, John Ruskin, whose cultural situation and training had ingrained the former into him but for whom the inspiring work of the artist William Turner encouraged the latter. In describing Turner as 'seizing the soul and the essence of beauty without regarding the means by which it is effected',[11] he touched upon that startling thrust of the artist's work which anticipated Modernism by half a century. In the earliest drawing of most untutored children, their natural priority prior to exposure to influence and tuition is similar: a direct expression of ideas through gesture from feeling.

Some research (initially that by James Sully around 1900) suggested that only a few successful artists revealed significant ability when young, and then mostly in adolescence.[12] But Sully and others were looking for the conventional observational drawing skills that most nearly reflected the academic style of their time. The nature of the drawings first formed by our seven artists might have placed them all outside the desired mode as embodied in Sully's research.

At first glance, Millais is an example of an artist whose early work, through his remarkable copying practices, might have signalled to Sully future eminence; yet it is the spontaneous sketches which seem more telling to a modern eye and without them the strength and individuality, as opposed to the imitative competence, of Millais' later work might never have appeared. Six of the seven (and possibly Millais too) started drawing in as directly expressive a manner as that employed by the mature Turner. However much they were conventionally trained later, it was the expressive impulse, important from an early stage, which made them into strong professionals. Constant

experiment imbued orthodoxy with the original vitality of the unorthodox.

Although Picasso felt particularly cheated by the loss (according to him) of an artistic innocence which ought to have preceded accommodation to convention, he had no eventual difficulty in subordinating those taught skills to his own ends. In spite of his protestations to the contrary, the evidence suggests a normal if accelerative child-like beginning to his drawing career, not unlike those of the other artists. His development is remarkable evidence for the formative importance of the earliest years.

An obsession with spontaneous drawing activity is undoubtedly an important indicator of future achievement, precisely because the volume and flexibility of practical experience from an early stage seems to be both common to many artists and also essential to the survival of drawing fluency in a pressurizing world. Skills of observation and copying have their value as disciplined visual and practical learning. Many individuals who never become (or wish to become) artists display such skills. The broader evidence suggests that such competence, although valuable in its own right, is rarely on its own an indicator of an artistic future, and it can sometimes be an impediment. It does indicate good visual analytical skill plus dexterity, both useful in art. But it lacks the boundary-breaking attitude necessary for artistic originality, which emerges from expressively spontaneous drawing, unimpeded by rules. All seven artists here found opportunities for spontaneous drawing, by concealment when necessary or, in the cases of Rothenstein and Raphael, without the need for it. Clues to the future are to be found more in the degree of imaginative invention of ideas and techniques than in any ability or desire to formalize them.

A third and subtle indicator of future potential concerns a tension between the expectations of the surrounding culture and the spontaneous artistic drive. Perhaps everyone experiences this tension, especially in adolescence, when imitating others, following trends and displaying accepted skills become issues big enough to erase individual approaches. But the seven artists here appear actually to have been stimulated by this tension and projected by it into new reactive strategies, essentially their own. This can be observed only in the attitudes represented in successive works by the same individuals, as opposed to single drawings – in changes of intention or method, in reinterpretations of earlier ideas and in the transformations of other people's conventions. These are the interactive expressions of the artist as a human being, responsive, creative and resilient, which transcend mere copying, manual dexterity and conformism.

While our seven artists present great differences of circumstances, experience and personality, they all thrived on this tension between what was expected of them and what they spontaneously produced. They appear to have matured as artists (of whatever kind) through the interaction between the two forms of experience, with their spontaneous, often highly inventive and unorthodox work providing the creative essence of their ultimate style.

Perhaps this tension, often provoked by the free and obsessive experiments of childhood, is the most vital phenomenon in the development of artistic skill and achievement. Those who do not manifest it remain art technicians, rather than empowered beings. The interaction of an early artistic 'innocence' and first experiences with the sophistication of later learning provides the alchemy to nourish the vision and the free imagination of the artist, whether the active professional or the one in us all.

Providing for the future artist

Public provision of education for those who reveal exceptional early ability in art is random or absent, depending on the educational policies of specific countries, which are related of course to economic factors at any given time and to the beliefs about the nature and value of art inherent in each culture. The chance factors of family circumstance, attitude and support are major determinants for good or ill in the development of artistic strengths, even when the obsession and the impulse are strong in themselves. While one feels that some highly exceptional individuals would have been unstoppable whatever the impediments and lack of support (Tom Phillips for example), others (such as Paul Klee or Sarah Raphael) might not have achieved as much as they have without a supportive ambience for their ability.

It is impossible to know how many individuals in any society have potential visual-expressive ability which is insufficiently, inappropriately or untimely nurtured or which perhaps just goes unrecognized. But just as there are those who have matured against the odds, whether early or late in life, and others who have faded as a result of unhelpful support, there are certain to be many with high potential which remains undeveloped. The natural activity of infant drawing is a clear indicator of the power of this expressive form and its universal relevance to human need.

A system for the avoidance of wasted potential in visual art – with all that that may mean for the cultural enrichment of societies as well as for individual lives and art itself – should be one which supports the conventionally able as well as the motivated and the obsessed, on the assumption that no clear dividing line exists between them. It is remarkable to find one of the most adequate models for this in the now-extinct Soviet regime. Their junior art schools (see p.12) and the post-*Glasnost* private Children's Academy in St Petersburg not only provide artist-tuition and sensitivity to the idioms of childhood and of adolescent art, but they also offer it to many who select themselves, whether or not they envisage a professional art career at the time.

There are lessons to be learned here, and also from examination of the development of artists, for the possibility of open public provision in other cultures. The need may be diverse: for some separately dedicated institutions, for others integrated into existing institutions and for a network of study opportunities available at any age. Above all there is a need for an empowering vision of the role of drawing and art in expression, a vision formed earlier by eminent educators such as John Ruskin, Viktor Lowenfeld,[13] Herbert Read and Marion Richardson,[14] but which has never been fully realized. In the encouragement of apparently exceptional individuals, this wider human context is important, in order to avoid the 'hothouse' unreality and the false self-image that can accompany early specialist provision, as well as to enrich the culture generally.

There are few countries which have pioneered early provision and some, like the United Kingdom, that have previously abandoned it. Parents who perceive unusual artistic fluency and commitment in their children should campaign in favour of it. But meanwhile they may be frustrated by their own inability to find the right course of action. Without professional advice, some draw upon their own (often inadequate) preconceptions of art, engaging tutors of limited worth or instituting a regime of intensive practice involving 'basic' but frequently inhibiting skills.

What can a parent do in this predicament? Seeking out professional rather than amateur artists and teachers would be one course of action, in order to obtain advice which is bedded in art, rather than in apocryphal notions about it; in no other field of study is it easier to be led astray. The studies of artistic development in this book show how the strongest future artists have focused intuitively on the expressive heart of artistic excellence rather than merely pursuing its tricks.

The seven artists examined in this book all related their work to the art they observed. Frequent contact with art of quality in major museums is a necessity, involving acts of comparison and contrast which avoid finite judgements. Opening up opportunities for individual interpretation is preferable to closing in on convention and conformity. Similarly the emerging artist's enthusiasm for imaginative experiment indicates a need for a rich diversity of materials and stimuli, but also the importance of not dictating approaches or methods.

The revelation here of the importance of spontaneous drawing, its scale and persistence, away from formal tutoring, is important to both parents and teachers, who otherwise judge performance only on a basis of overt activity. While the spontaneous work may initially be private, adults need to demonstrate wherever possible their respect for and interest in this work as a significant, even central, part of the whole activity.

In summary, professional advice where it can be found: constant association with good art and intensive but essentially free experiment, along with the provision of opportunity, in terms of space, materials and time, seem the most likely effective strategies for nourishing and developing artistic ability to the point where the public or private educational system takes over, whenever that is. The task is not to discipline the obsession or to cultivate impressive performance in any one direction, but to nurture it broadly and freely.

Neither is it wise to project every action towards an imagined future of eminence and fortune. Perhaps the most important discovery from this study of some children who were to become artists is the extent to which in their spontaneous earliest work they were actively exploring their feelings, coping with distress, celebrating pleasures, understanding complexities and evolving ideas. It is imperative to understand that prolific drawing activity can serve those sorts of immediate needs in everyone, in childhood and adolescence, as well as contributing towards eventual artistic achievement.

Visual expression for all

This investigation of the emergence of seven artists has encouraged in me the view that artists' experience can have value and meaning for others, even though lifelong preoccupation with the practice of art may not be a feature of their lives. It is common in discourse to use one sensory mode to explain something about another; there is taste in music, rhythm and melody in visual images. Remarkable are the parallels between Patsy Rodenburg's perceptions about the role and development of speech as balancing and enriching an individual's life, and those which may also be advanced for visual and artistic expression: children 'speak in order to know the world ... Those of us who don't talk about our experience often find ourselves cut off from it.'[15] Like the voice, the eyes need to be trained; visual

skills require active development and sometimes remedial treatment. Artistic expression, like expression through speech, represents and interprets ideas, though visually rather than aurally. Poor habits or inhibitions can also hinder visual learning and expression. Yet, as with the voice, the capacity to think, to imagine and to express visually is essential to fulfilment as an individual.

No one could reasonably argue that successful visual artists (any more than good actors) are somehow quite different from or more perfect than others because they have these special fluencies. The biographies of some artists are full of awkward emotional and social difficulties and flawed personalities, all of which may be more visible in them but no greater than in the human condition generally. The drawing histories of those studied here are remarkable for their similarities in terms of interest and application, even if not of pace, invention and sheer persistence. Artists in general are less impeded by external influences and their energies are more focused than those of others. These are strengths which are open to development rather than unique attributes which cannot be acquired.

The seven artists' shared impulse to draw was clearly inseparable from their existence as individuals in a complex and challenging world and was fuelled by a passionate search to understand it through a visual medium. The need for visual understanding is universal and the potential of drawing for us all is ably demonstrated by visual artists and many young children; everyone has such a need and *initially* attempts its fulfilment.

Early drawing activity seems to be potentially formative for everyone of later ideas, not only about art. Copying and style-adoption could be widely useful in skill development; sufficient diversity of prepubertal drawing experience, inventive in subject-matter, technique, style and intention, could help avoid the impasse of adolescent inhibition in drawing and sustain its expressive role. But just when most children begin to weaken in their drawing fluency as other cultural pressures on them grow, we have tended to deflect their energy into other activities where their performance at the time seems stronger. It is at this stage that further encouragement to draw, freedom to experiment and the stimulus of the example of the work of a variety of art and artists could sustain their interest, impetus and natural expressive inclination.

In the curricula of many modern countries there is evidence of a diminishing concern for individuality, expression and the arts. This process needs to be turned around, by acknowledging the case for sensitive and timely nurturing of drawing and other natural skills of expression which are a need and a right. One

38 Sacks 1995, pp.231–32.

39 Gillberg and Coleman 1992, p.43; see also Wing 1981.

40 Ford 1991, p.104.

41 Freeman 1984, p.109.

42 Noy 1972, p.243.

43 Thomas 1961, pp.44–53.

44 Barnes 1992, p.28.

45 Storr 1988, p.75.

46 In Rachel Barnes, 'Horn of Plenty', *Guardian*, October 1994.

47 Gooding 1994.

48 In an interview with William Feaver, 'The Artist out of his Cage', *Observer*, 6 December 1992.

49 Geidion-Welcker 1952, p.8.

50 Paine 1985, pp.303–27.

51 Howe 1993.

52 Schapiro 1979, p.82.

53 In an interview with Bill Hurrell, *Modern Painters*, Winter 1992.

3 Academic training and an independent attitude

1 Millais 1979.

2 Warner 1979, pp.5–16.

3 M. Warner in Paine 1981, p.9.

4 Frith 1887.

5 Ibid., p.33.

6 Leslie 1914, p.36.

7 Morgan 1968, pp.48–58.

8 Ibid., p.123.

9 Ibid.

10 Ibid., p.25.

11 Ibid., pp.113–14.

12 Warner 1979, pp.11–14.

13 Millais 1979.

14 Frith 1887.

15 Warner 1979, p.22.

16 Paine 1981, no.38.

17 Wilton and Lyles 1993, pp.14–17.

4 Privilege, opportunity and misfortune in the making of an artist

1 Dortu 1971. References to drawings by the young Toulouse-Lautrec in this chapter are often by 'D' + a number, referring to this catalogue.

2 Goldschmidt and Schimmel 1969, p.33.

3 Ibid., p.41.

4 Marks 1972, p.139.

5 Andrew Mortimer in conversation with the author, 1985.

6 John Russell 1965, p.23.

7 Goldschmidt and Schimmel 1969, pp.29–31.

8 Quoted in ibid., p.34.

9 Ibid., pp.38–39.

10 Ibid., p.45.

11 Ibid., p.49.

12 Vignaud de Villefort 1973, p.8.

13 Goldschmidt and Schimmel 1969, p.46.

14 Ibid., pp.53–56.

15 Ibid., p.57.

16 Ibid., p.15.

17 Ibid., pp.59–60.

18 Thomson 1977.

19 Joyant, M., *Henri de Toulouse-Lautrec*, vol.1, Floury, Paris 1926, pp.43–4, quoted by Thomson in Paine 1981.

20 Thomson, p.14.

21 Ibid., p.101.

5 Early ambition and a vision of artistic nobility

1 Richardson 1991, p.13.

2 See for example Gedo 1972, p.8.

3 Penrose 1958, p.275.

4 Richardson 1991, p.29.

5 Ashton 1972, p.75.

6 Gedo 1972, p.3.

7 Richardson 1991, p.3.

8 Gedo 1972, p.4.

9 Walther 1994.

10 Ibid., p.36.

11 Here and in later references to works by Picasso, 'MBP' indicates the work's number in the Museo Picasso, Barcelona; 'MP' indicates a number in the Musée Picasso, Paris.

12 Stassinopoulos-Huffington 1989.

13 Richardson 1991, p.29.

14 Museo Picasso catalogue 1985, p.43.

15 Richardson 1991, p.48.

16 Read 1943, p.125.

17 Ashton 1972, p.56.

18 Richardson 1991, p.52.

19 Ibid., p.55.

20 Ibid., p.61.

21 Vallentin 1963, p.9.

22 Richardson 1991, p.74.

23 Ibid., p.14.

24 Ibid., p.16.

25 Vallentin 1963, p.8.

26 Ibid., p.7.

27 Ibid., p.2.

28 Richardson, BBC2, 14 February 1994.

29 Walther 1994, p.49.

30 Stassinopoulos-Huffington 1989, p.19.

31 Gedo 1972, p.9.

32 Ibid., p.11.

33 Vallentin 1963, p.3.

34 Richardson 1991, p.27.

35 Stassinopoulos-Huffington 1989, p.20.

36 Gedo 1972, p.14.

37 Ibid., p.5.

38 Ibid.

39 Richardson 1991, p.33.

40 Quoted in ibid., p.67.

41 Ibid., p.25.

6 A savage and gentle passion

1 Much (but not all) of this work is now in the Art Education Centre at Drumcroon, UK.

2 Rothenstein undated.

3 From an interview by the author with Michael Rothenstein, October 1988 (hereafter 'Interview 1988').

4 Rothenstein, interview 1988.

5 Rothenstein undated.

6 Interview 1988.

7 Ibid.

8 Ibid.

9 Rothenstein undated.

10 Interview 1988.

11 Bryan Robertson, obituary of Michael Rothenstein, *Independent*, 9 July 1993.

12 Interview, 1988.

13 Mel Gooding, obituary of Michael Rothenstein, *Guardian*, 9 July 1993.

14 Interview 1988.

15 Ibid.

16 Robertson obituary 1993.

17 Interview 1988.

18 Interview with Peter Fuller, *Modern Painters*, 3(4), Winter 1990–91.

19 Interview 1988.

20 Rothenstein 1993.

21 Interview 1988.

22 Ibid.

23 Ibid.

24 Ibid.

25 Ibid.

26 Waldemar Januszczak, in *Modern Painters*, 1(4), Winter 1988–89, p.77.

27 Interview 1988.

7 The young humorist

1 Most of these early drawings are now in the possession of Mrs Annetta Hoffnung, wife of the artist.

2 References to catalogue numbers and titles for some of the sketches in this chapter are to the unpublished catalogue of the 1978 exhibition 'Childhood to Maturity'; see Bibliography.

3 A. Hoffnung ed. 1960, p.99.

4 Ibid., p.101.

5 Ibid., p.116.

6 Feaver 1981.

7 A. Hoffnung ed. 1960, p.116.

8 In A. Hoffnung 1988.

9 Ibid., p.14.

10 G. Hoffnung 1957.

11 Ibid.

12 A. Hoffnung 1962.

13 Ibid.

14 G. Hoffnung 1955.

15 G. Hoffnung 1956.

8 A professional journey

1 James 1992.

2 Borchgrave 1992.

3 Interview with the author, one of several. Later quotes from the artist in this chapter are also from a series of interviews with the author.

4 Sylvia Raphael in an interview with the author.

5 Osborne 1987.

6 Boyd 1995.

9 Displacing the demon

1 Downes 1993.

2 Ibid.

3 Ibid.

4 In interview with the author; quotes later in this chapter not from Downes's MA dissertation come from a series of interviews with the artist and his family.

5 A reference to the title of his MA dissertation, Downes 1993.

10 Sustaining expression through drawing

1 Paine 1985, pp.327–40.

2 See for example Paine 1992, pp.1–13.

3 Rodenberg 1992.

4 Rousseau 1982 (1762), p.31.

5 Paine 1985, pp.303–27.

6 Alan Davie, in a video autobiography shown at the Royal West of England Academy, October 1992.

7 B. and A. Wilson 1977.

8 Frith 1887.

9 Howard Hodgkin, BBC Radio 4, 28 November 1994.

10 Greer 1981.

11 Ruskin, *Works*, vol.III, p.639.

12 See for example Sully 1895.

13 Lowenfeld 1958 (1947).

14 See for example the Marion Richardson archive at the Department of Art Education, University of Central England, Birmingham.

15 Rodenberg 1992, p.40.

16 For a discussion of the importance of 'feeling' as playing a 'supreme part in the ordering and disciplining of human understanding', see L. A. Reid, in Smith 1970, p.76.

17 Klee means by this 'unfettered by convention', not 'unaided'.

18 Paul Klee, in 1914, quoted in Andrew Hagan.

Bibliography

Ariès, P., *Centuries of Childhood*, London: Penguin Books, 1973 (first publ. 1960).

Arts Council of Great Britain, *The Drawings of John Everett Millais*, exhibition catalogue, preface by Joanna Drew, 1979.

Ashton, Dore, *Picasso on Art: a Selection of Views*, London: Thames and Hudson, 1972.

Barnes, R., ed., *Matisse* (Artists by Themselves), London: Bracken Books, 1992.

Barron, F., *Artists in the Making*, New York: Seminar Press, 1972.

Berenson, B., *Italian Painters of the Renaissance*, London: Phaidon, 1959.

Berlin, Sven, *Alfred Wallis 1855–1942: a Primitive*, London: Nicholson and Watson, 1949.

Blunt, Anthony, and Phoebe Pool, *Picasso: The Formative Years*, London: Studio Books, 1962.

Borchgrave, Helen de, 'Sarah Raphael', *Arts Review*, February 1992.

Boyd, William, Introduction to *Sarah Raphael, Desert Paintings*, exhibition catalogue, London: Thos. Agnew and Son, 1995.

CIBA Foundation, *The Origins and Development of High Ability, a Symposium*, London, 1993.

Clark, G. A., and E. Zimmerman, *Resources for Educating Artistically Talented Students*, Syracuse NY: Syracuse University Press, 1987a.

— *Issues and Practices Related to Identification of Talented Students in the Visual Arts*, National Research Centre for the Gifted and Talented, Stoors, CT, 1987b.

Copeland, Aaron, *Music and Imagination*, London: Oxford University Press, 1952.

Csikszentmihalyi, M., and J. W. Getzels, 'The Personality of Young Artists: an Empirical and Theoretical Exploration', *British Journal of Psychology*, 64(1).

Curtis, Tony, *Welsh Painters Talking*, Cardiff: Poetry Wales Press Ltd, 1997.

Dali, S., *The Diary of a Genius*, London: Hutchinson, 1964.

Darwin, C., 'A Biographical Sketch of an Infant', *Mind* II, 1877.

Dortu, M.-G., *Toulouse-Lautrec et son Œuvre*, New York: Collectors Editions Ltd, 1971.

Downes, David, 'Disordered Development', unpublished MA dissertation, Brighton Polytechnic, 1993.

Feaver, William, *Masters of Caricature*, London: Weidenfeld and Nicolson, 1981.

Fein, Sylvia, *Heidi's Horse*, California: Axelrod Press, 1976.

Fineberg, Jonathan, *The Innocent Eye: Children's Art and the Modern Artist*, Princeton NJ: Princeton University Press, 1977.

Ford, Boris, 'Floating Boy', *Modern Painters*, 4(2), Summer 1991.

Freeman, Joan 'Talent in Music and Fine Art', *Gifted Education International*, 2, 1984.

Frith, W. P., *My Autobiography and Reminiscences*, vol.1, London: Richard Bentley and Son, 1887.

Gardner, H., *Artful Scribbles*, London: Jill Norman Ltd, 1980.

— *Creating Minds*, USA: Basic Books, 1993.

Gedo, John, 'On the Psychology of Genius', *International Journal of Psychoanalysis*, 53, April 1972.

Geidion-Welcker, C., *Paul Klee*, London: Faber and Faber, 1952.

Gillberg, C., and M. Coleman, *The Biology of the Autistic Syndromes*, New York: Mackeith Press and Cambridge: Cambridge University Press, 1992.

Goldschmidt, L., and H. Schimmel, eds, *Unpublished Correspondence of Henri de Toulouse-Lautrec*, London: Phaidon, 1969.

Gooding, Mel, 'Plastic Writing', review of the exhibition 'Drawing the Line', *Royal Academy Magazine* (London), 47, Summer 1995.

Greenacre, Phyllis, *Emotional Growth: Psychoanalytic Studies of the Gifted and a Great Variety of Other Individuals*, New York: International University Press, 1971.

Greer, Germaine, *The Obstacle Race*, London: Pan Books Ltd, 1981 (first publ. 1979).

Hagan, Andrew, *Klee's Development*, catalogue of the Paul Klee Collection of the Guggenheim Museum, New York, 1993.

Hauser, Arnold, *The Social History of Art*, London: Routledge and Kegan Paul, 1951.

Hoffnung, A., *Hoffnung, his Biography*, London: Gordon Fraser, 1988.

— ed., *O Rare Hoffnung*, London: Putnam and Co. Ltd, 1960.

Hoffnung, G., *The Hoffnung Symphony Orchestra*, London: Dobson, 1955.

— *The Hoffnung Music Festival*, London: Dobson, 1956.

— *Hoffnung's Acoustics*, London: Dobson, 1959.

— 'Childhood to Maturity: the Early Drawings of Gerard Hoffnung', unpublished catalogue of an exhibition in the Institute of Education Gallery, University of London, 1978.

Howe, M., 'The Early Lives of Child Prodigies', paper delivered at the CIBA symposium, London, 1993.

— *Fragments of Genius*, London: Routledge, 1989.

James, Clive, Introduction to *Sarah Raphael, 1989–1991*, exhibition catalogue, London: Thos. Agnew and Son, 1992.

Janssen, R. and J., *Growing Up in Ancient Egypt*, London: The Rubicon Press, 1990.

King, James, *Interior Landscapes: a Life of Paul Nash*, London: Weidenfeld and Nicolson, 1987.

Langer, Suzanne, *Philosophy in a New Key*, London: Harvard University Press, 1957.

Leslie, G. D., *Inner Life of the Royal Academy*, London: John Murray, 1914.

Lowenfeld, Viktor, *Creative and Mental Growth*, New York: Macmillan, 1958 (first publ. 1947).

Luquet, G., *Les Dessins d'un enfant*, Paris: Librairie Felix Alcan, 1913.

MacDonald, Stuart, *The History and Philosophy of Art Education*, London: University of London Press, 1970.

Malraux, André, *Saturn: an Essay on Goya*, London, 1957.

Marks, Claude, *From the Sketchbooks of the Great Artists*, New York: Thomas Cromwell and Co., 1972.

Marland, S. P., *Education of the Gifted and Talented: Report to the Congress of the United States by the U.S. Commissioner of Education*, vol.I, Washington DC: US Government Printing Office, 1972.

Millais, Geoffroy, *Sir John Everett Millais*, London: Academy Editions, 1979.

Moholy-Nagy, S., *Paul Klee: Pedagogical Sketchbook*, London: Faber and Faber, 1968 (first publ. 1925).

Morgan, H. C., 'A History of the Organisation and Growth of the Royal Academy to 1836', unpublished MA dissertation, University of Leeds, 1964.

Mullins, Edwin, *Alfred Wallis: Cornish Primitive*, London: Pavilion Books, 1994.

Murray, P. and L., *The Penguin Dictionary of Art and Artists*, Harmondsworth: Penguin, further revised edn, 1968.

Museo Picasso, *Catálogo de Pintura y Dibujo*, Ajuntament de Barcelona, 1985.

Noy, Pinchas, 'About Art and Artistic Talent', *International Journal of Psychoanalysis*, 53, April 1972.

Ochse, R., *Before the Gates of Excellence*, Cambridge: Cambridge University Press, 1990.

Osborne, H., *The Oxford Companion to Art*, Oxford: Oxford University Press, 1987.

Paine, S., 'The Development of Drawing in the Childhood and Adolescence of Individuals', unpublished Ph.D thesis, London University, 1985.

— 'Child's Play', *New Society*, 31 October 1986.

— 'The Demise and Possible Rise of Early Specialist Education in Art', *Journal of Art and Design Education*, 8(3), 1989.

— 'Conflicting Paradigms of Vision in Drawing Development Research', in D. Thistlewood, ed., *Drawing Research and Development*, UK: Longman Group, 1992.

— 'Ruskin and Recent Controversy on the Teaching of Drawing to the Young', unpublished paper delivered to the Conference 'Ruskin and Art Education Today', Sheffield, October 1996.

— ed., *Six Children Draw*, London: Academic Press, 1981.

Palau i Fabre, Joseph, *Child and Caveman: Elements of Picasso's Creativity*, London: Academy Editions, 1978.

Pariser, D., 'The Juvenile Drawings of Klee, Toulouse-Lautrec and Picasso', *Visual Arts Research* (USA), 13, 1987, pp.53–57.

— 'Social and Cultural Influences on the Childhood Drawings of Klee, Toulouse-Lautrec and Picasso', paper presented at the Society for Research in Child Development, Baltimore, 1987.

Penrose, Roland, *Picasso: his Life and Work*, London: Granada, 1958 (first publ. 1958).

Phillips, Tom, *Works and Texts*, London: Royal Academy of Arts/Edition Hansjorg Mayer, 1992.

— 'Music in Art', *BBC Music* Magazine, December 1994.

Pickvance, R., *The Drawings of Gauguin*, London: Paul Hamlyn, 1970.

Piironen, Lisa, ed., *The Power of Images*, Finland: INSEA, 1992.

Radford, John, *Child Prodigies and Exceptional Early Achievers*, UK, Harvester and Wheatsheaf, 1990.

Raphael, Sarah, *Sarah Raphael, 1989–1991*, exhibition catalogue, London: Thos. Agnew and Son, 1992.

— *Desert Paintings*, exhibition catalogue, London: Thos. Agnew and Son, 1995.

Read, Herbert, *Education through Art*, London: Faber and Faber, 1970 (first publ. 1943).

Reiss, S., *The Child Art of Peggy Somerville*, London: The Herbert Press, 1990.

Richardson, John, *A Life of Picasso*, vol.1, London: Jonathan Cape, 1991.

Rodenberg, Patsy, *The Right to Speak*, London: Methuen, 1992.

Rothenstein, M., *Looking at Paintings*, London: Routledge, 1947.

— *Personal Writings*, London: Redstone Press, 1993.

— 'Messages from the Hand', unpublished text, undated; photocopy in the possession of Mrs Sam Rothenstein.

Rousseau, J., *Emile*, trans. Barbara Foxley, London: J. M. Dent, 1982 (first publ. 1762).

Royal Academy Commission Report 1863

Ruskin, J., *The Works of John Ruskin*, vol.III (*Modern Painters*, vol.I), London: George Allen, 1903.

Russell, B., *The Autobiography of Bertrand Russell, 1914–1944*, vol.LI, London: Oxford University Press, 1968.

Russell, John, *Seurat*, New York: Oxford University Press, 1965.

Sacks, Oliver, *An Anthropologist on Mars*, London: Picador, 1995.

Salome, R. A., 'A Limited Summary of Research on the Artistically Gifted', *Translations: From Theory to Practice*, 2(1), 1992.

San Lazzaro, G. di, *Klee, a Study of his Life and Work* (trans. Stuart Hood), London: Thames and Hudson, 1957.

Schapiro, Meyer, *Modern Art of the 19th and 20th Centuries*, New York: George Braziller, 1978.

Selfe, Lorna, *Nadia*, London: Academic Press, 1977.

Smith, Ralph, ed., *Aesthetic Concepts and Education*, University of Illinois Press, 1970.

Stallworthy, J., *An Anthology of Poems written in Childhood and Youth*, Oxford: Oxford University Press, 1988.

Stassinopoulos-Huffington, A., *Picasso, Creator and Destroyer*, London: Pan Books Ltd, 1989.

Storr, Anthony, *The School of Genius*, London: André Deutsch, 1988.

Sully, James, *Studies of Childhood*, London: Longmans, Green and Co., 1895.

Szatmari, P. *et al.*, 'A Follow Up Study of High-Functioning Autistic Children', *Journal of Autism and Development Disorders*, 19, 1989, pp.213–25.

Thomas, D., 'Poetic Manifesto' (from a letter), *Texas Quarterly*, 4, 1961, pp.44–53.

Tomlinson, R. R., *Children as Artists*, London: King Penguin, 1944.

Thomson, R., *Toulouse-Lautrec*, London: Oresko, 1977.

Vallentin, Antonina, *Picasso*, London: Cassell, 1963.

Vasari, G., *The Lives of the Artists*, London: Penguin Classics, 1965 (first publ. 1550; revised edn 1568).

Vignaud de Villefort, Mme du, 'Autour de Toulouse-Lautrec', *Extrait du Bulletin de la Société des Sciences, Arts et Belles Lettres du Tarn*, 1973.

Wallas, D., and H. Gruber, *Creative People at Work*, New York: Oxford University Press, 1989.

Walther, Ingo F., *Pablo Picasso 1881–1973*, vol.1, Cologne: Benedict Taschen, 1994.

Warner, M., 'Millais as a Draughtsman', in the catalogue of the Arts Council of Great Britain exhibition *The Drawings of John Everett Millais*, 1979.

Whalley, J. I., *Beatrix Potter, 1886–1943: the Artist and her World*, London: F. Warne and Co., 1987.

Wilson, B. and M., 'Iconoclastic Views of the Imagery Sources in the Drawings of Young People', *Journal of the Art Education Association*, 30(1), January 1977.

Wilton, Andrew, and Anne Lyles, 'Ambition and Ambiguity', introduction to the catalogue *The Great Age of British Watercolours 1750–1850*, Munich: Prestel, 1993.

Wiltshire, Stephen, *Floating Cities*, London: Michael Joseph, 1991.

Wing, Lorna, 'Asperger's Syndrome: a Clinical Account', *Psychological Medicine*, 1981.

Index